Theology Today
28 The Theology of Original Sin

D1482400

Theology Today

GENERAL EDITOR
EDWARD YARNOLD, S. J.

No. 28

The Theology of Original Sin

BY

EDWARD YARNOLD, S. J.

distributed by
CLERGY BOOK SERVICE
HALES CORNERS, WISCONSIN

Nihil obstat:
Jeremiah J. O'Sullivan, D. D.
Censor Deputatus
6 August 1970

Imprimatur:
† Cornelius Ep. Corcag. & Ross
9 September 1971

cum licentia superiorum ordinis

SBN 85342 278 8

To Jean, Joe and the Family

ACKNOWLEDGEMENTS

The Scripture quotations in this publication, unless there is indication to the contrary, are taken from the Revised Standard Version of the Bible, copyrighted 1946 and 1952 by the Division of Christian Education of the National Council of Churches of Christ in the U.S.A. and used by kind permission. The quotation from the article of my late friend and master, Fr. B. Leeming, is printed by kind permission of the author and the Editor of *Clergy Review*. *The Dead Sea Scrolls in English,* by G. Vermes, is quoted by kind permission of the author and Penguin Books Ltd. (Translation copyright © G. Vermes, 1962).

ABBREVIATIONS

Dz: H. Denzinger & A. Schönmetzer, *Enchiridion Symbolorum, Definitionum et Declarationum* (33rd edit., Barcelona etc., 1965)
PL: Migne, *Patrologia Latina*
PG: Migne, *Patrologia Graeca*

CONTENTS

PREFACE

Man is haunted by two spectres: the sense of individual guilt and the awareness that the whole race has suffered a fall.

That everyone experiences a sense of personal guilt is commonplace. The conviction that the whole race is sick is scarcely less widespread. The Greeks had their legend of the lost Golden Age. Dualistic religions, like those of the Gnostics or the Manichees, taught that life is a conflict between a good and an evil principle; spirit is the creation of the good god, matter of the bad; man is a spirit imprisoned in a material body and struggling to get out. Cardinal Newman recorded how he came to the conclusion that the aimlessness of life was inexplicable without a doctrine of a Fall:

> To consider the world in its length and breadth, its various history, the many races of man, their starts, their fortunes, their mutual alienation, their conflicts; and then their ways, habits, governments, forms of worship; their enterprises, their aimless courses, their random achievements and acquirements, the impotent conclusion of long-standing facts, the tokens so faint and broken of a superintending design, the blind evolution of what turn out to be great powers or truths, the progress of things, as if from unreasoning elements, not towards final causes, the greatness and littleness of man, his far-reaching aims, his short duration, the curtain hung over his futurity, the disappointments of life, the defeat of good, the success of evil, physical pain, mental anguish, the prevalence and intensity of sin,

the pervading idolatries, the corruptions, the dreary hopeless irreligion, that condition of the whole race, so fearfully yet exactly described in the Apostle's words, 'having no hope and without God in the world', – all this is a vision to dizzy and appal; and inflicts upon the mind the sense of a profound mystery, which is absolutely beyond human solution. What shall be said to this heart-piercing, reason-bewildering fact? I can only answer, that either there is no Creator, or this living society of men is in a true sense discarded from His presence... And so I argue about the world; – if there be a God, since there is a God, the human race is implicated in some terrible aboriginal calamity. It is out of joint with the purposes of its Creator. This is a fact, a fact as true as the fact of its existence; and thus the doctrine of what is theologically called original sin becomes to me almost as certain as that the world exists, and as the existence of God (*Apologia,* Chapter 5).

Arthur Koestler, looking with a biologist's eye at the anomalies in man's make-up, reached a similar conviction which he expressed in scientific rather than religious terms:

The evidence seems to indicate that at some point during the last explosive stages of the evolution of *homo sapiens* something has gone wrong; that there is a flaw, some subtle engineering mistake built into our native equipment, which would account for the paranoid streak running through our history (*The Observer,* 28th September 1969).

The feeling of individual guilt and the conviction that the whole race has fallen are the experiences which find their true explanation in the Christian doctrines of personal and original sin. Although this book deals with personal sin in Part I, its main theme is original sin in

10

Part II. This plan has not been adopted because the theology of personal sin is slight, but simply because original sin is the more controversial topic, and therefore needed a more fully argued treatment.

I wish to express my thanks here to my friends who read sections of the book in draft and helped me to avoid several errors: Dr Gerhardt May, Fr John Russell, Fr Ian Brayley, Fr Francis Laishley and Fr Anthony Meredith, of whom the last four are all colleagues in the Society of Jesus.

Part I

Personal Sin

At the beginning of the Mass the priest says: 'To prepare ourselves to celebrate the sacred mysteries, let us call to mind our sins'. Why should we?

Because the fact that Jesus saves us from our sins is the most important thing we need to know about him. His name was chosen to express this: 'You shall call his name Jesus, for he will save his people from their sins' (Mt 1.21; cf. Lk 1.31; 2.21); 'Jesus' means 'the Lord saves'. The angel announced the Nativity to the shepherds in similar terms: 'To you is born this day in the city of David a Saviour' (Lk 2.11). St John the Baptist was a witness to the same truth: 'Behold, the Lamb of God, who takes away the sin of the world' (Jn 1.29). For St Paul liberation from sin is the essential achievement of the Resurrection: 'If Christ has not been raised, your faith is futile and you are still in your sins' (1 Cor 15.17). Acknowledgment of one's sin is an essential duty for the Christian: 'If we confess our sins, he is faithful and just, and will forgive our sins and cleanse us from all unrighteousness. If we say we have not sinned, we make him a liar, and his word is not in us' (1 Jn 1.9, 10). We do not understand our relationship with Christ, unless we see him as 'the expiation for our sins' (1 Jn 4.10). Christianity, therefore, is a religion of salvation and redemption; but redemption and salvation cannot be understood without reference to sin.

It is this last point that many people, especially today, find difficult to accept. They say they do not experience

13

sin in themselves, although the denial of the fact of sin does seem peculiarly perverse when recent history and contemporary events afford spectacular examples of mass genocide, racial hatred, exploitation of the poor, the torture of prisoners and profiteering by the sale of hard drugs.

There are several reasons why people take up this paradoxical position in face of the all too apparent manifestation of sin:

(1) Psychological reasons. A man's motives and choices, it is said, are determined by his circumstances and his character, and his character itself is the product of heredity and environment; free will is an illusion, and so is the sense of guilt. But a clear distinction must be made between guilt-feelings and genuine guilt. Guilt-feelings may indeed be irrational and frequently harmful; but this fact does not prove that there is no such thing as objective guilt, that I am never free enough to be responsible for my own shortcomings.

(2) Sin is taken to mean the violation of an external, and even arbitrary, rule of conduct. Bad preaching must carry much of the blame for this misconception. The results are drastic: once people come to see (as St Paul did) that virtue cannot be merely a matter of keeping rules, even divine rules (for then it develops into self-righteousness), and that sin cannot be merely the breaking of rules (for then God becomes a taskmaster), they naturally tend to reject the whole notion of sin.

(3) Reasons based on a naive optimism. It is morbid to dwell on my failure, it is said; it is more constructive to concentrate on my potentiality. Or: Christianity is a religion of love, not of guilt. Or: it is healthier to speak of the limitations of human nature rather than of sin; we may not love as much as we ought, but we love as much as we can. Or: I can never assess the extent of my guilt (which is true), so it is better to ignore it (which is a

non-sequitur). Such reasons lack logical force, but they appear to exert an influence in many people's minds.

Yet despite this reluctance to make much of sin, people feel a great sensitivity to social sins, i.e. injustices in the social system; hence the frequency of public protests. However, the contradiction is less marked than at first sight appears. We understand more vividly than past generations our involvement with the community, and we have expanded our idea of community to cover the whole world; but we have become less sensitive to our own personal guilt. We are more prepared to say, 'Society is at fault', than we are to say '*I* have sinned'.

There is no answer on the level of logic to this tendency to reject the existence of sin. You cannot prove to a person that he is a sinner, that his sense of guilt is not always illusory. The ultimate reason for accepting the fact of sin is faith: to deny it is to deny redemption, and therefore to deny Christianity, to 'make Christ a liar'.

Sin is the rejection of God, the refusal to love him. But in this life people do not, at least normally, indulge in pure hatred of God; when God is rejected it is because of selfishness. It would be misleading to say 'because of self-love', for proper self-love is psychologically, and perhaps logically, necessary in all our choices. Love is a relationship of the self with another, not the annihilation of self; Christ's follower is to love his neighbour *as himself* (Mt 22.39), as Christ has loved him (Jn 13.34). Proper self-love is open to others, and therefore to God; the sinner shuts himself off from others, and therefore from God. Pride, the ultimate in this atomic selfcentredness, is therefore the ultimate sin. Goodness, on the other hand, is summed up in the double love of God and neighbour; all other obligations are simply the practical demands of this double love. 'On these two commandments depend all the Law and the prophets' (Mt 22.36-40).

15

Just as love of God needs to be made actual in love of neighbour, so sin, the focussing of love exclusively inwards on the self, never occurs in this life in a naked form; it too needs to be realized, to become incarnate, so to speak, in particular decisions and acts which amount to a rejection of what love demands here and now. It is at this point that law comes in. The moral law is simply a series of generalized statements about the way in which love of God, and therefore love of neighbour, is correctly realized in practice. If I really love, this is the right way to show it, because this is what human needs require. The moral law is a natural law; that is, it follows from the needs of human nature. It is not a set of arbitrary rules. Consequently, sin is not the failure to observe a rule, but the refusal to meet the practical demands of love.

It follows that the *damage* done by sin consists in this objective element, the failure to do as the situation demands. For this reason the intellectualist Socratic view of sin is correct as far as it goes: sin is always a 'mistake', the unintelligent course, just as much as when a doctor prescribes the wrong drug. But the *moral evil* of sin consists in the subjective state, the ill-will of the sinner, the turning in on self to the exclusion of genuine love of God and neighbour. Both objective and subjective elements are important: it is ruinous to be correct in action but evil in intent, and also ruinous to have good intentions but to act in the wrong way. It is this need to get the answer right that explains why ascetical writers attach such great importance to self-examination. To try to assess my degree of subjective guilt is often futile and morbid; but I need to be continually checking myself to see if my acts are objectively right, if I am doing what the needs of others require.

We have seen that normally in this life a human choice is not an uncomplicated rejection or acceptance

16

of God. Such states of mind do exist in heaven or hell: there is a connection between the single-mindedness of such choices and their permanence. God does not need to imprison sinners in hell; they are their own hell; they are no longer capable of changing their mind and repenting, any more than a saint in heaven is capable of sinning. Their will is fixed, for good or evil, totally and irrevocably. Perhaps in extremely rare cases a sinner may reach this irrevocable rejection of God even on earth. This seems to be the frame of mind which the New Testament describes as the unforgivable or 'mortal' sin:

> Whoever blasphemes against the Holy Spirit never has forgiveness, but is guilty of an eternal sin (Mk 3.29). There is sin which is mortal; I do not say that one is to pray for that. All wrongdoing is sin, but there is sin which is not mortal (1 Jn 5.16-17).

By 'mortal' sin St John does not mean what is normally described in this way today, i.e. grave sin which can be forgiven. It will be better, therefore, to call what St John has in mind 'fatal' sin. Since God's mercy is inexhaustible, sin can be fatal only if it makes the sinner incapable of receiving the grace of repentance, so that he shuts himself up exclusively and definitively in his self-centredness, and his hell begins on earth.

Apart from this extremity of sin, there are two other kinds of sin, mortal and venial. It is correct to call them 'kinds' rather than 'degrees' of sin, because they represent two totally different conditions. A man who commits a mortal sin rejects God fundamentally, shuts himself off deliberately at the deepest level from the love of God and neighbour; he divests himself of all charity, and therefore all grace, and expels God from his dwelling within him. Such a one has deprived himself of the power of repentance, but unlike the man who commits the 'fatal' sin, is still capable of responding to the grace of repentance when God offers it. He is not yet completely hardened and completely blind. Although mortal sin lacks the finality of the 'fatal' sin, it requires a high degree of clarity and deliberateness. Naturally, however, this clarity and deliberateness need not be expressed explicitly in theoretical terms in the sinner's mind. One can commit a mortal sin without saying to oneself, 'I am committing a mortal sin'; otherwise mortal sin would be possible only for a person with some theoretical knowledge of moral theology.

Venial sin is a totally different kind of sin. It does not involve the fundamental and deliberate rejection of God. The person who commits such a sin remains basically united to God in love, retains his share in God's nature and God's presence within him, is still a son of God and a brother of Christ. He remains, that is to say, in a state of grace. But still he refuses to make the claims of love absolute; despite his basic 'Yes' to God and neighbour, he utters a more superficial 'No'. A person in venial sin can be compared to a boy who has disobeyed or offended his father. He knows he has not totally damaged his relationship with his father, that his father will continue to love him and care for him; but he has weakened the relationship of trust and love between them.

The relationship, then, that a venial sinner has towards God is totally different from that of a mortal sinner. This distinction has so far been explained in subjective terms as a difference of moral state in the sinner. This is the essential distinction. But there is also a difference at the objective level. One cannot separate oneself entirely from God over a purely trivial matter; nor can one fully deliberately omit to do a serious thing which love demands without cutting oneself off from God. It is in this sense that the moral theologians distinguish between serious and light matter. But, of course, it does not follow that to commit a sin concerning serious matter always involves subjective mortal sin or *vice versa*. I

18

may be totally or partially ignorant; I may not be totally free; indeed it seems likely that the subjective conditions for mortal sin are relatively rarely fulfilled. It also seems possible that, though a demand love makes on me may be in itself trivial, I may perceive so clearly that it completely epitomizes my ideals that to refuse to meet the demand would entail the total rejection of God. This possibility appears to be confirmed by our Lord's account of the Last Judgment (Mt 25.31 ff.) and the parable of Dives and Lazarus (Lk 16.19 ff.), where the sins of the damned do not appear, taken separately, to be particularly great. Many a confessor might say that such a refusal to give alms involved only light matter.

This emphasis on the subjective element in distinguishing between mortal and venial sin may appear to open the door to scruples. It implies that it is an oversimplification to conclude that, because there is no grave matter, the sin is 'only' venial. And since it is difficult to assess the subjective element, it follows that one can be much less certain that a sin is not mortal than is normally supposed. In fact it seems to be an article of the faith that one cannot be totally sure if one is in mortal sin or not. The Council of Trent declared:

> Anyone who considers himself and his own infirmity and weakness can be anxious and fearful about his grace, since no one can know with the infallible certainty of faith that he has received God's grace (Dz 1534).

The force of this teaching becomes clearer in the light of another distinction that has to be drawn. Sin can be considered as an act or as a state. By a mortally sinful *act* I deprive myself of my state of sanctifying grace and put myself in the *state* of mortal sin. This state continues until I answer God's invitation to repentance, i.e. until by the help of actual grace I make an act of perfect contrition or validly receive the sacrament of penance. As long as I remain in this state of mortal sin I am incapable of an act which has value in God's sight, as all such acts, being supernatural, presuppose the state of grace which I have lost. I may continue to perform objectively good acts, but subjectively they cannot be acts of love as long as I remain in the loveless state of mortal sin. It follows, therefore, that I cannot tell with complete certainty that I am in a state of grace on the strength of any objectively good acts I may perform.

In this last sentence the operative words are 'with complete certainty'. The application of our Lord's principle, 'You will know them by their fruits' (Mt 7.16), can give me practical certainty, certainty enough to allow me to receive Holy Communion, but I always *might* be mistaken. Are the fruits really good?

We may experience in our lives a sense of peace and union with Christ which seems to be an awareness of grace. The experience may come in prayer, in the generous quality of our everyday lives, or in some important decision we make in which we put the interests of others before our own. But even here we *might* be mistaken. People are, after all, sometimes led to the contrary mistake, when their feelings of guilt convince them they are cut off from God: the interpretation of religious experience (what St Ignatius called 'discernment of spirits') is not always easy. We have the certainty we need for day-to-day living, but we *might* be wrong.

And this brings us to the heart of the matter. I can never rely on my own achievements. I am never entitled to address God from a position of strength, as the Pharisee thought he could. Not only are all my merits the work of God's grace; not only am I continually failing to love God as much as I ought and could, and so committing venial sin; but I can never be wholly sure that I am in a state of grace at all. I cannot trust myself; I have to put all my trust in God – not in God's goodness in rewarding me for my merits, but in his mercy in forgiving my sins. The basic Christian attitude we have already described as a sense of sin; another way to describe it is a sense of inadequacy. But the Christian's sense of guilt and inadequacy is not depressing or debilitating, because he knows that despite his guilt and inadequacy he is accepted by the only one whose acceptance ultimately matters. In the knowledge that I am accepted by God I can come to accept myself.

This self-acceptance, of course, does not provide an excuse for complacency and sloth. If I learn to accept my failings because God in his mercy accepts them, I will go on trying to correct them, or at least to make good in another way the damage they cause. T. S. Eliot prayed for this combination of self-acceptance and the attempt to improve:

Teach us to care and not to care

Teach us to sit still *(Ash Wednesday).*

Christianity is a religion of redemption, salvation, liberation. It would be possible to have a religion in which we were taught our limitations and learnt to accept them because God valued our limited capabilities. But that is not Christianity. Christianity teaches us that, even though we are united to God by grace, we are repeated failures; that we have to appear with our failure and guilt before the penetrating gaze of him who 'is like a refiner's fire' (Mal 3.2), who loves us so much that he will not be content with anything less than what is best for us; that he forgives us over and over again, not with the supine complaisance of a vapid weakling, but with the love of a father who will be demanding, even apparently harsh, in his determination to bring the best out of us. Christianity requires that we accept forgiveness. To do this wholeheartedly is the complete victory over self-centredness.

Part II

Original Sin

CHAPTER I

THE PROBLEM

The Christian's deeply-felt conviction that the human race is a society of sinners is not derived only from his knowledge of the sins he has himself committed, nor from the all too cogent evidence that others sin like himself. There exists, and not only among Christians, a conviction that man is flawed even before he himself has chosen to sin; he belongs to a race that carries a collective guilt, has suffered a collective perversion, a fall from the moral integrity that is both his due and duty, so that in his individual experience he is constantly aware of a force that pulls him down from his ideals, a short-fall between his higher, real self, and the imperfect way in which he manages to express that real self when it comes to putting ideals into practice. St Paul gave classical expression to this feeling of self-dissatisfaction:

We know that the law is spiritual; but I am carnal, sold under sin. I do not understand my own actions. For I do not do what I want, but I do the very thing I hate. Now if I do what I do not want, I agree that the law is good. So then it is no longer I that do it, but sin which dwells within me. For I know that nothing good dwells within me, that is, in my flesh. I can will what is right, but I cannot do it. For I do not do the good I want, but the evil I do not want is what I do. Now if I do what I do not want, it is no longer I that do it, but sin which dwells within me. So I find it to be a law that when I want to do right, evil lies close at hand. For I delight in the law of God, in my inmost self, but I see in my members another law at war with the law of my mind and making me captive to the law of sin which dwells in my members (Rom 7. 14-23).

The traditional Catholic experience of this conviction is as follows: God endowed the first human beings, Adam and Eve, with privileges which their descendants were to inherit. They were free from the gravitation away from the good which we have just been describing, and which theologians call concupiscence, without referring particularly to sex. They were not liable to death, toil and pain. These gifts were enhancements of man's natural capacities ('preternatural', – *beyond,* but on a level with, nature – is the technical term). But above all, they enjoyed a privilege which was so great that it cannot be considered merely as man's existing capacities raised to the *n*th degree (as if a man were enabled to run at sixty miles an hour); it is rather something of a totally different order from man's capacities (as if a chimpanzee were enabled to create original poetry or to make a scientific discovery). Indeed this crowning privilege was utterly beyond the capacities of any being God could create. (Theologians describe it as 'supernatural' – *above* nature). It consisted in the share in God's nature, the faculty of familiar intercourse with God, that we are accustomed to call 'sanctifying grace'.

But Adam and Eve sinned, and as a consequence lost these privileges not only for themselves but for their descendants. They, and we, their successors, like them, became liable to pain, toil and death:

> In pain you shall bring forth children... In the sweat of your face you shall eat bread till you return to the ground, for out of it you were taken; you are dust and to dust you shall return (Gen 3.16,19).

They, and we, forfeited that moral equilibrium which was the original endowment of the race. Above all each human being enters into the world without grace, and consequently in a state of alienation from God which can accurately be described as 'sin'.

But God's Son became man and died and rose again in order to save man not only from his personal sins, but also from this original sin. This salvation is applied to each person at baptism. But if anyone, even a baby, dies without baptism (or at least the equivalent of a desire for it), he is not saved from this original sin, remains separated from God, and consequently cannot enjoy God's presence in heaven. The baptized, on the other hand, at once receive sanctifying grace, the share in God's nature, but remain liable to pain and death, and to the experience of the inclination towards sin.

Such is the understanding of the doctrine of original sin which was almost invariably held by Catholics until a very few years ago. It is, however, open to several serious objections:

1. *Moral objections.* The separation from God, or absence of grace, is described as 'sin'; indeed, the old catechism up till recently in general use in England called it 'the guilt or stain on the soul which was inherited from Adam'. But how can sin or guilt be inherited? They are essentially personal, a burden freely assumed by the individual, his very own revolt against God. It simply does not make sense to say that all subsequent generations are guilty of Adam's sin, and to that extent are themselves sinners.

The reply might be made that this talk about the inheritance of guilt or sin is simply a figure of speech. Only Adam and Eve were guilty of their sin. But subsequent generations have to share the punishment for that sin, though not the guilt. This solution therefore avoids the nonsense of inherited guilt, but it still implies something which seems almost as nonsensical – that the just God can punish people for the sins of others. It is no answer to point out that the same thing happens in law; when a man is put into prison, his wife and children suffer for his crime, however much a welfare state tries to help them economically. This is no answer, because the sufferings of the criminal's dependants are not regarded as punishments that they have to undergo; on the contrary, we do all we can to cushion them, precisely because they are not to blame. Whereas if you hold that God punishes the whole human race for the sin of its founder, you are implying that God purposely contrived a punishment for the innocent, when he could easily have limited the ill-effects to the guilty partners, Adam and Eve.

These 'moral' objections appear with particular force in the case of babies who die without baptism, and consequently without the capacity to attain, either explicitly or implicitly, to faith in Christ and desire of baptism. It is true that the child would not suffer, but would simply remain on the natural level, unable to feel any sorrow at the loss of something which it is beyond its powers even to imagine, for one does not miss what one cannot know. Nor indeed need one think that the mother would be *away* from her child; there seems to be no reason why they should not be together, with the mother enjoying supernatural happiness while the child is content with its fill of natural happiness. Father B. Leeming, S. J., paints in warm-hearted terms a picture of these unbaptized babies in their state of natural happiness:

The picture of Limbo should rather be of children, themselves happy as their little hearts can wish, and rejoicing in the happiness of others, but not pining for the precise kind of happiness which others have. None of the blessed in heaven feels unhappy because he has not the degree or the kind of glory which others enjoy. Unbaptized infants may be considered as having as much happiness as the heart of man can conceive, and as lacking only the happiness which it is beyond the heart of man to conceive... For all we know, they may play a precious role in revealing God's goodness and love in a way which others do not, just as those lower in glory reveal God's goodness in a different way from those higher in glory (*Clergy Review* 39 (1954) pp. 68-69).

But even if Limbo is described in these humane terms, even if it is admitted that no one has the right to heaven, many find it hard to believe that God should make the eternal destiny of babies who die depend on mere good fortune. Father Leeming is, of course, as sensitive to this problem as anyone. For an attempt to explain how unbaptized babies can be saved the reader is referred to No. 25 in the *Theology Today* series, *The Theology of Baptism* by Sister L. Brockett.

2. *'Physical' objections*. In earlier times writers exercised their ingenuity to conceive ways in which original sin might have been handed down, generation by generation, from Adam to their own times. St Augustine, for example, thought it possible that in conception the father sowed the seed of the soul as well as of the body; original sin could then be regarded as an hereditary defect passed on from Adam to subsequent generations (*Contra Julianum Pelagianum,* V. iv. 17; PL 44.794). In the same passage St Augustine refers to another explanation

which was more commonly held, namely that it is the body which bears a genetic flaw inherited from Adam: the soul, though directly created by God and not descended from the first man, nevertheless contracts the original flaw from the corrupt body in which it is contained. There was a third material explanation that St Augustine was driven to adopt by the pressures of his uneasy controversy against the Pelagians: because conception necessarily involves sinful passion, the child from the very beginning of its existence carries a moral flaw. St Augustine's reputation has suffered in modern eyes as a result of this third theory, but in fact he did not invent it: it can be traced back to his elder contemporaries Hilary of Poitiers (315-367) and Ambrose (c. 339-397), and even to Origen in the third century (cf. p. 60f.). Ambrose connects this theory with the virgin birth of Christ: if Christ had been born of a human father and mother, his body would have been 'besmirched' by the 'harmful linking of generation and conception' (De Paenitentia, 1.3.13; PL 16.470).

The naive terms in which these theories are framed should not blind us to what is a genuine problem: how did Adam's sin change the human constitution so radically as to make man subject to pain, death and concupiscence? How can a sin, which is in the moral order, change the physical as well as the psychological pattern not only of the sinner but also of his descendants? Of course sin, such as drug-taking, can have permanent physical and psycho-physical effects which lead to moral ruin; but it is not the moral factor, the sinfulness itself, that causes the ruin. Now, no one supposes that original sin is the inherited physical or psycho-physical effect of some material and corrupting self-indulgence on Adam's part: according to any exposition of the doctrine it is the moral factor, the sinfulness itself, the disregard of God's law, not the material element, the object that is wrong-

28

fully chosen (the forbidden fruit) that causes the ruin of the whole race. And if the physical defects of man's nature, especially death and pain, are inexplicable in this way, so too is the psychological defect, concupiscence. It is difficult to believe that the first human beings could make a choice so traumatic in its effects that the psychological equilibrium even of their posterity could be radically disturbed by it. How can death, pain and concupiscence have arisen from Adam's sin? Are we reduced to regarding them as arbitrary sanctions imposed by a vindictive God?

The objection can be pressed further. Even if it were granted that Adam's sin could have had some effect on the physical and psychological constitution of the whole race, it would still be scarcely credible that there could be the particular effects in question, involving as they do such a radical alteration in man's nature. A human being who could not die or feel pain and had complete self-mastery would be virtually a different species. To speak of an immortal human being with a body that cannot suffer and a will that is drawn solely by its true good is almost a contradiction in terms; such a creature would be so different from us that it could hardly be called human at all. For there to be no sensitivity to pain, no gradual wearing out of the bodily organs leading to death, no psychological conflict, the physical and mental constitution would have to be totally different. Moreover, it is difficult to imagine what growth of character would be possible in conditions from which all sources of challenge had been removed.

To sum up the 'physical' objections, it is inconceivable that Adam's sin could have had these effects, and equally inconceivable that the flawless human life that is postulated could ever have existed.

3. *Biological objections.* As I have no scientific compe-

tence, I must confine myself to retailing arguments which I am myself not qualified to assess.

At the centre of the traditional view that we are examining critically is the belief that the whole human race descended from a single pair of ancestors. This view is called monogenism, to distinguish it from polygenism, the theory that states that the species must have sprung from more than one pair. The reasons for rejecting monogenism are as follows:

(a) The unit of evolution seems always to be not a single *pair* but an evolving population, a *group* of interbreeding individuals. It is hard to envisage any genetic mechanism which would produce a single pair of a new species and then stop short.

(b) If only a single pair did evolve, there would be a persistent genetic weakness through a number of generations. To survive and meet the hazards to which it was exposed, the new human species would need a much larger stock of inheritable variations than could be supplied by a single couple.

It seems therefore that a form of polygenism is demanded by the scientific evidence. Some biologists hold the human race evolved from several points of origin at different places and at different times. This form of polygenism is called ployphyletism. The more common view is that the anatomical and physiological variations are small enough to allow descent from a single group at a single place and time; indeed, it is argued that the probability of the evolutionary process repeating itself with a different group is extremely low. Most biologists, therefore, accept a theory of monophyletic polygenism, maintaining that the whole human race throughout the world evolved from a single population in one region.

Clearly, all these biological objections can be met by an appeal to a special intervention by God. This appeal is an ace of trumps; of course, God has the power to intervene, and it cannot be proved that he did not use it. One can only question whether it would be characteristic of God to go about things in this way. Our experience of his action in the world in our own time suggests that he respects his creation so much that he allows it to proceed according to its own 'laws'. Of course, there are ways in which God can be said to 'intervene'. There has been one transforming intervention by God, the Incarnation. There is God's constant providential guidance of history in accordance with the 'laws' by which his creatures exist, and not in violation of them. God intervenes again at the conception of every human being, as each soul, being spiritual, is God's special creation; but this repeated creative activity is demanded by man's nature, and is not a series of adjustments of the laws of nature or a suspension of them. Again, it is an historical fact that God does sometimes, in a very few particular cases, for the good of an individual, interfere with the normal processes of nature; when he does so we say he has worked a miracle. But although there have been all these different kinds of intervention by God, the particular form of intervention postulated to explain the origin of man would appear to be characterized by singular inconsistency and arbitrariness on God's part. It would be implied that God created the world with a tendency to evolve towards man, its highest species, but chose to modify that tendency in order to make a single couple the source of the whole race. Why should he do this, if not to make Adam's choices influence the future of all the race – in which case the 'moral' arguments apply with especial force, as the situation would be one of God's own choosing?

4. There is another anomaly implied by the traditional view; it might be called the *'epistemological'* objection. Granted the *truth* of the tradition, how did we come to

know it? We derive it, of course, from Genesis, but how did the author of this part of the Pentateuch (known as the Yahwist) learn of it? There seem to be only two possible explanations, neither of which is satisfactory. The first is that there was an unbroken oral tradition to this effect going back for hundreds of thousands of years to Adam. That such a tradition could be preserved accurately seems unlikely; it is known, for example, how Christians cut off for a couple of hundred years from priests and without books seem to lose knowledge of even the most basic facts of Christianity, though they preserve sacred names and ceremonies. But even if the tradition of man's origin could have been maintained, how did Adam himself learn that he was to be the ancestor of all human beings? The second possible explanation is simply that God miraculously enlightened the mind of the Yahwist, or of the writers from whom he derived his material, concerning the origins of the human race. This explanation is, of course, theoretically possible, but one can only say again that such action is not according to God's style. Scripture scholars have in recent years gained much information about the way in which the biblical authors derived their ideas from existing documents or from the beliefs of neighbouring peoples. Indeed, many would say that biblical inspiration is very largely God's providential guidance as it brings a writer of a particular character into contact with a particular complex of intellectual influences (see *The Theology of Inspiration* in this series). It seems therefore that whatever interpretation we should put on Genesis 1-2 – and this question will be raised again in the next chapter – we should not take it as an historically accurate account of the origins of man.

To sum up, in this chapter we have marshalled several serious objections against the traditional way in which original sin is explained. Personally I find them in combination convincing. Two possibilities therefore remain. Either the doctrine of original sin should be altogether rejected, or the 'traditional' explanation of it should be discarded and another substituted. The former solution seems impossible for one who believes in the infallibility of the Church. Our next step, therefore, must be to examine scripture, the Fathers and the official teaching of the Church to see how far they support the 'traditional' explanation.

CHAPTER II

SCRIPTURE

The three main sources in scripture for the doctrine of original sin are Genesis, the Wisdom Books and St Paul.

(1) *Genesis*

It is now generally agreed by Old Testament scholars that the Pentateuch is a composite work made up of a number of different interwoven traditions of varying dates. One of these traditions, known as the Yahwistic source, is recognisable by the characteristic use of the name Yahweh to describe God, and is thought to have been recorded in writing in the ninth century B.C. In the first eleven chapters of Genesis several episodes taken from the Yahwistic source have been included which are connected with the origin of sin.

The first and best-known of these is contained in the story of the fall of Adam and Eve. It is, however, misleading to describe the episode in these terms, as 'Adam', unlike 'Eve', is not a proper name, but simply means 'Man'. This fact immediately opens the door to the conjecture that the author may not in fact be intending to describe a particular historical figure, the first man, but rather a symbolic 'Everyman'.

The Yahwist includes several important details in his account of the state of happiness in which the Man lived before his fall. He had access to the tree of life (2.9) and was immune from death (2.17). He had mastery over the animals (2.19-20) and enjoyed the fruits of the earth (2.15). Nakedness caused him no shame (2.25). This last point should perhaps be seen not precisely as a proof of sexual innocence but rather as the ability to make straightforward and uncomplicated relationships with others; for, as the incidents of Noah's drunkenness and David's dance indicate (Gen 9.21; 2 Sam 6.20), after the Fall nakedness is seen not so much as a cause of lust, as a source of shame in both the naked one and those who see him.

Man's sin caused him to lose all these blessings. He was expelled from Eden and denied access to the tree of life (3.23-24). He became liable to death (3.19). He forfeited his mastery over nature and now could wrest a livelihood from the soil only by the grind of hard work (3.17-19). He became aware and ashamed of his nakedness (3.7-10); this awareness is the consequence of eating fruit from the tree of the knowledge of good and evil. Woman, instead of being man's partner and helper (2.18, 24), becomes his inferior and subject to the pains of childbirth (3.16).

In the previous chapter we have argued that the account of the Fall in Genesis is not an attempt at literal reporting of an historical fact. It is rather what is known in the technical terminology of anthropology as a myth. This use of the word does not imply that the story is simply a fictitious legend; the meaning is that a truth too deep for straightforward expression is formulated in

34

symbolic terms, here the terms of a story. Whether the author believed in the literal meaning of the story is not the point; the point is that the story is used principally as an expression of a more important truth.

The Yahwist adopted his story of the Fall of Man from Mesopotamian sources. Scholars are not in complete agreement about the truth that he was using these symbols to express. Some maintain that Adam, Everyman, is invented to illustrate the sinfulness of each of us; the evil in the world is due not to God but to man; as Adam sinned, so do we. If this interpretation is true, the author has no intention of speaking of a doom which the whole human race contracts from the sin of the first man.

However, this interpretation does not take into account the contrast between man's state before and after the Fall. It seems preferable, therefore, to take the story as an attempt to explain in symbolic terms the existence of evil in man's condition; why is man a prey to death, pain, toil and mistrust? The serpent stands for another cause of sorrow in man's experience: perhaps man's sexual passion or his ambition which encourages him to violate God's law. The Yahwist's answer is that, as the cause cannot be God, it must be man himself and his vulnerability to forces outside him; it was sin that disturbed the orginal harmony of creation.

This philosophy of life implies that the *consequences* of the original sin are inherited by subsequent generations; but it does not follow that what is inherited is *guilt* or *punishment*. Nevertheless it was a common Hebrew belief that guilt and punishment could spread from the individual sinner to his race, his family and his descendants. Thus God makes the Israelites suffer a defeat in war in punishment for the sin of one individual, Achan, and gives Joshua this explanation:

Israel has sinned; *they* have transgressed my covenant which I commanded them; *they* have taken some of the devoted things; *they* have stolen and lied (Jos 7.11).

The concept of inherited guilt was summed up in the proverb: 'The fathers have eaten sour grapes, and the children's teeth are set on edge.' But the prophets, in their attempt to lead the Israelites to a more refined moral consciousness, denied the proverb's truth (Jer 31.29-30; Ezek 18.24). Still, even Jeremiah did not completely discard belief in inherited punishment, and even perhaps inherited guilt; the following passage seems both to accept and reject the idea:

Nothing is too hard for thee, who showest steadfast love to thousands, but dost requite the guilt of fathers to their children after them..., rewarding every man according to the fruit of his own doings (Jer 32.17-18).

The Baptist scholar, H. Wheeler Robinson, spoke in this connection of the concept of 'corporate personality'. In Hebrew law and custom an individual could put his whole group under a liability; this is the explanation of blood-feuds and the obligation of a dead man's brother to marry the widow if she had borne no sons. By a similar process of thought a messianic figure like the Son of Man (Dan 7) or the Suffering Servant (Is 53) will apparently stand for both an individual and the whole messianic race.

In the third chapter of Genesis, then, the Yahwist is probably expressing his belief that the evils in the human condition are the consequence of the sins of earlier generations, or even of the first man; probably, too, he sees the consequences as inherited *punishment* due to the whole human race for the sins of an ancestor. In the subsequent chapters, in a series of further episodes, the same author works out his theology of sin in greater breadth.

36

The incident of the murder of Abel shows how succeeding generations not only suffered the consequences or punishment of Adam's sin, but themselves fell before temptation. Even before the murder Yahweh tells Cain, who is resentful at the rejection of his sacrifice:

'If you do well, will you not be accepted? And if you do not do well, sin is couching at the door; its desire is for you, but you must master it' (Gen 4.7).

Presumably because of Adam's sin, his descendants have become vulnerable to temptation, though they have the power to overcome it.

The Yahwist relates another Fall-story at the beginning of the sixth chapter in terms of the mating of the sons of God with the daughters of man. Later Jewish and Christian writers generally took the sons of God to be the angels, but this interpretation cannot be proved from the biblical text. Whether the episode was originally a different account of the origin of sin, or whether it represents only one further stage in the spread of sin, the author adds a new item to the catalogue of suffering in Chapter Three. Man is now not only liable to death, but his life is to be limited to 120 years (Gen 6.3).

The book of Genesis continues with the Yahwist's introduction to the story of the Flood.

The Lord saw that the wickedness of man was great in the earth, and that every imagination of the thoughts of his heart was evil continually (Gen 6.5).

He decides, therefore, to wipe out the human race by a flood, with the exception of Noah and his family. When the flood subsides the Lord is appeased by Noah's sacrifice, and makes this promise:

'I will never again curse the ground because of man, for the imagination of man's heart is evil from his youth; neither will I ever again destroy every living creature as I have done' (Gen 8.21).

By these words the author marks a change of mind on God's part; God now decides that he must make allowances for man's 'evil imagination', as man simply cannot help experiencing it. His heart is evil 'from his youth'; his wicked inclination precedes his personal sins, and therefore he is not to blame for it. The Yahwist does not, however, consider the origin of this tendency to evil: is it due to man's nature or to Adam's sin?

The last Fall-story in this part of the Bible is the story of the Tower of Babel. The sin of the inhabitants of Babel seems to be pride and ambition, which Yahweh takes as an attack on his own supremacy:

> Then they said, 'Come, let us build ourselves a city, and a tower with its top in the heavens, and let us make a name for ourselves, lest we be scattered abroad upon the face of the whole earth'... And the Lord said, 'Behold they are one people, and they have all one language; and this is only the beginning of what they will do; and nothing that they propose to do will now be impossible for them. Come, let us go down, and there confuse their language, that they may not understand one another's speech.'... And from there the Lord scattered them abroad over the face of all the earth (Gen 11.4-9).

This story is designed to show how man's sin is responsible for another of the evils of man's existence, namely his geographical and linguistic divisions. (The Holy Spirit at Pentecost removes the language-barrier: Acts 2.6.)

To sum up, the Yahwist's Fall-stories are for the most part myths he has adapted in order to show that it is man's own sin that is responsible for the various evils of human life: death, suffering, divisions, woman's inferior status and the universal tendency to evil. This doctrine implies the solidarity of the human race; it is not the individual's own sins that bring these evils upon him, but the sins of his ancestors.

(2) *The Wisdom Books*

The later books of the Old Testament do not always adhere to this philosophy of life. In particular, death is often taken as a necessary, unalterable fact of man's existence, rather than a consequence of his sin. The prophet's picture of the new age, free from distress, injustice and conflict with nature, does not represent man as immortal, but as immune from *premature* death:

> For behold, I create new heavens
>> and a new earth;
> and the former things shall not be remembered
>> or come into mind...
> I will rejoice in Jerusalem
>> and be glad in my people;
> no more shall be heard in it the sound of weeping
>> and the cry of distress.
> No more shall there be in it
>> an infant that lives but a few days,
>> or and old man who does not fill out his days;
> for the child shall die a hundred years old,
>> to fall short of a hundred years shall be
>> reckoned a curse (Is 65.17-20; RSV version
>>>>> changed in last line).

Not all writers, however, can accept the fact of death so joyfully; some see it as a tragic necessity to be accepted only with resignation:

> Lord, let me know my end,
>> and what is the measure of my days;
>> let me know how fleeting my life is!...
> Surely every man stands as a mere breath!
>> Surely man goes about as a shadow!
> Surely for nought are they in turmoil;
>> man heaps up and knows not who will gather!
> And now, Lord, for what do I wait?
>> My hope is in thee (Ps 39.4-7).

There is not yet belief in an after-life: death is the final separation from God. Affliction and premature death is a punishment for one's own sins or those of one's ancestors; prosperity and long life is a reward for virtue.

> Yet a little while, and the wicked will be no more;
>> though you look well at his place, he will not be there.
> But the meek shall possess the land,
>> and delight themselves in abundant prosperity
>>> (Ps 37.10-11).

The theme of man's evil heart is frequently developed.

> The heart is deceitful above all things, and desperately corrupt;
>> who can understand it? (Jer 17.9)
> A new heart I will give you, and a new spirit I will put within you; and I will take out of your flesh the heart of stone and give you a heart of flesh (Ezek 36.26).

Man suffers from this tendency to sin from the very beginning of life; it is an inherited disposition:

> Behold, I was brought forth in iniquity,
>> and in sin did my mother conceive me (Ps 51.5).
> The wicked go astray from the womb,
>> they err from their birth, speaking lies (Ps 58.3).
> Who can bring a clean thing out of an unclean?
>> There is not one (Job 14.4).

No-one succeeds in mastering this tendency to evil; all choose to sin:

> They have all gone astray, they are all alike corrupt,
>> there is not one that does good,
>> no, not one (Ps 14.3).
> If thou, O Lord, shouldst mark iniquities,
>> Lord, who would stand (Ps 130.3)?
> We have all become like one who is unclean,
>> and all our righteous deeds are like a polluted garment.
> We all fade like a leaf

40

and our iniquities, like the wind, take us away (Ps
64.6).

Although in many of these passages the tragic elements
of man's condition were connected with sin, whether it is
the sin of the sufferer or that of his ancestors, they were
not linked with the story of Adam until the Wisdom
Books were composed in post-exilic times. The author of
Ecclesiasticus seems to put all the blame squarely on
Eve's shoulders:

From a woman sin had its beginning,

and because of her we all die (25.24).

Both sin and death, therefore, come from the first
woman. However, we should not take these words as a
cool and scientific theological statement. They form the
climax of the extended blast of the trumpet against the
monstrous regiment of women in which the author in-
dulges his misogynism:

The wickedness of a wife changes her appearance,

and darkens her face like that of a bear...

A sandy ascent for the feet of the aged –

such is a garrulous wife for a quiet husband (25.17,
20).

In fact, Adam and Eve have only a minor place in Ben
Sirach's thinking. In Chapter 44 he begins a eulogy of
'famous men' in chronological order, but starts with
Enoch, not Adam. It is not till the end of the list that
perfunctory acknowledgement is made of Adam's unique
position:

Shem and Seth were honoured among men,

and Adam above every living being in the creation
(49.16);

and even here he may not be speaking of Adam, but
simply of 'man' in general. He has much to say about
death, but links it with the sin in Paradise only in the
one passage already quoted. In his fairly lengthy account of creation (16.26-17.11), he seems to believe that

41

from the beginning God 'gave to men few days, a limited time' (17.2), and there is no suggestion that the harmony of creation was upset by a Fall. Indeed one receives the impression that this passage is intended as a counterblast to Gen 3; what the Yahwist regards as evils caused by Adam (whether he is intended as a representative symbol or an historic person), Ben Sirach regards as natural to men and no reason for distress. Thus, knowledge of good and evil is not a consequence of Adam's sin but a gift of God:

> He filled them with understanding
>> and showed them good and evil (Ecclus 17.7).

The tendency to evil is a greater source of bewilderment to Ben Sirach. He refrains from linking it with ancestral sin:

> O evil inclination, why were you formed
>> to cover the land with deceit (37.3)?

The author of Ecclesiastes had earlier put the blame on man:

> Behold, this alone I found, that God made men upright, but they have sought out many devices (7.29).

There is evident in the Wisdom books a tendency to extend the significance of death. Some of the ideas of the earlier books of the Old Testament are vigorously repeated in this connection. Thus, though death is natural to man, it comes untimely and violent to the sinner:

> With all flesh, both man and beast,
>> and upon all sinners seven times more,
> are death and bloodshed and strife and sword,
>> calamities, famine and affliction and plague.
> All these were created for the wicked,
>> and on their account the flood came (Ecclus 40.8-10)

Children can suffer because of their fathers' sins:

> The inheritance of the children of sinners will perish,

and on their posterity will be a perpetual reproach (Ecclus 41.6).

What is new in the Wisdom books is the belief that death is not only the end of life, perhaps a consequence of sin, but has an affinity with sin. This can perhaps be seen already in Ben Sirach, with his simple division of the fruits of life into the good and the evil:

Good is the opposite of evil
    and life the opposite of death;
    so the sinner is the opposite of the godly.
Look upon all the works of the Most High;
    they are likewise in pairs, one the
    opposite of the other (Ecclus 33.14-15).

The Wisdom of Solomon, the last of the Wisdom books, which dates from the first century before Christ, works out the connection between sin and death in much greater detail. There is now a belief in an after-life in which the unjust are filled with 'anguish of spirit' while the righteous man is 'numbered among the sons of God', with 'his lot among the saints' (Wis 5.3, 5). Death is not God's work but the devil's, and towards it all sinners tend:

Do not invite death by the error of your life,
    nor bring on destruction by the works of your hands;
    because God did not make death,
    and he does not delight in the death of the living.
For he created all things that they might exist...
    and the dominion of Hades is not on earth.
For righteousness is immortal.
But ungodly men by their words and deeds summoned death;
    considering him a friend they pined away,
    and they made a covenant with him,
    because they are fit to belong to his party...
For God created man for incorruption,
    and made him in the image of his own eternity,

43

but through the devil's envy death entered into the world,
and those who belong to his party experience it.

(Wis 1.13-16; 2.23-24).

The author evidently means by death something more than the end of life on this earth, for the just also are liable to death in this sense, even an untimely death:

The righteous man, though he die early, will be at rest.

For old age is not honoured for length of time (4.7-8).

Early death and suffering can both be means by which God prepares the just for the reward in the next life:

Having been disciplined a little, they will receive great good,
because God tested them and found them worthy of himself;
like gold in the furnace he tried them,
and like a sacrificial burnt offering he accepted them

(3.5-6).

The death, then, which the wicked consider their friend and to whose party they belong, must be something more than physical death; it includes both the spiritual death of a sinner in this world, and his punishment in the next. But the death of the just is not really death at all; he lives with God:

The souls of the righteous are in the hand of God,
and no torment will ever touch them.

In the eyes of the foolish they *seemed* to have died,
and their departure was *thought* to be an affliction,
and their going from us to be like a destruction,
but they are at peace...

Their hope is full of immortality...

The faithful will abide with him in love (3.1-4, 9).

Love of her [wisdom] is the keeping of her Laws
and giving heed to her laws is assurance of immortality,

and immortality brings one near to God (6.18-19).

The author of Wisdom also deals with the evil imagination, seeing it as the effect of environment rather than an inner force. God makes the just man die young so as to save him from this contaminating influence:

He was caught up lest evil change his understanding or quite deceive his soul.

For the fascination of wickedness obscures what is good,

and roving desire perverts the innocent mind (4.11-12).

This contagion spreads especially within a family: the wives of the ungodly are foolish, and their children are wicked (3.12).

Unlike Ben Sirach, the author of Wisdom ascribes to the first man a role in the history of sin, although he is not given the proper name Adam. He is at least the first in the series of sinners:

Wisdom protected the first-formed father of the world,

when he alone had been created;

she delivered him from his transgressions,

and gave him strength to rule all things (10.1-2).

What is emphasized here is not the catastrophic effect of Adam's sin, but his repentance and the restoration of his powers over nature. It is the sins of subsequent generations that bring their own ruin:

But when an unrighteous man departed from her in his anger,

he perished because in rage he slew his brother.

When the earth was flooded because of him, wisdom again saved it,

steering the righteous man by a paltry piece of wood (10.3-4).

God made man 'for incorruption... in the image of his own eternity', but at a point in history (presumably

Adam's sin) through the devil's envy death entered the world' (2.23-24). Adam's sin, then, opens the gate to let death, both physical and spiritual, enter the world and spread.

To sum up, Ecclesiasticus and Wisdom depict a world which has fallen from its original immortality, and is now liable to death in its fullest sense. This fall is the result of sin, beginning with that of the first man. Man's evil inclination is generally accepted unquestioningly as a fact of life, though the sin of others at least contributes to its growth. We have here, then, a doctrine of the inherited evil consequences of sin, which the individual aggravates for himself by his own sins.

(3) *St Paul*

The Gospels do not throw any direct light on original sin; our main source for this doctrine in the New Testament is St Paul. Before we examine his epistles, however, it will be illuminating to try to discover how contemporary Jews thought about the problem.

We have already considered some evidence which dates from not long before St Paul's time, namely the book of Wisdom, written in the first century B.C. The *Community Rule* (or *Manual of Discipline*), one of the Dead Sea Scrolls, which antedates Wisdom by a few decades, develops the theory of the evil imagination (Gen 6.5; cf.p.). It is God who has established the bad as well as the good spirit in man; sin therefore consists not only in experiencing the evil spirit but in giving way to it:

The nature of the children of man is ruled by these [two spirits], and during their life all the hosts of men have a portion in their divisions and walk in [both] their ways. And the whole reward for their deeds shall be, for everlasting ages, according to whether each man's portion in their two divisions is great or small. For God has established the spirits in equal measure until the final age, and has set everlasting hatred between their divisions (CR IV, trans. G. Vermes, p. 77).

The Ethiopic *Book of Enoch,* written about the same time as the *Community Rule,* puts the emphasis rather on man's freedom:

As a mountain has not become a slave and a hill does not become the handmaid of a woman, even so sin has not been sent upon earth, but man of himself has created it, and under a great curse shall they fall who commit it (ed. Charles, 98.4).

The *Apocalypse of Baruch* (first century A.D.) introduces Adam into its account of sin; but Adam is only the first sinner of a series, not the cause of the sin and death of his posterity:

For though Adam first sinned and brought untimely death upon all, yet of those who were born from him each one of them has prepared for his own soul torment to come... *Adam is therefore not the cause, save only of his own soul, but each of us have been the Adam of his own soul* (ed. Charles, 54.15ff.).

Some decades later the Fourth Book of Ezra combines this view that each individual re-enacts Adam's choice for himself with the opinion that Adam is responsible for the presence of the evil heart in each member of the race:

For the first Adam, clothing himself with the evil heart, transgressed and was overcome; and likewise also all who were born of him. Thus the infirmity became inveterate; the Lord indeed was in the heart of the people, but with the evil germ; so what was good departed and evil remained... And after this had been due many years, the inhabitants of the City committed sin, in all things doing even as

Adam and all his generations had done: *for they also had clothed themselves with the evil heart* (ed. Charles, 3.20ff.). A grain of evil seed was sown in the heart of Adam from the beginning, and how much fruit of ungodliness has it produced unto this time and shall yet produce till the threshing-floor come (4.30).

Consequently, when we turn to St Paul we shall expect to find him teaching that Adam has been the source of sin and death in two ways: as the *example* which later generations follow, thus bringing death on themselves, and as the *cause* of the 'evil heart' (the tendency to sin) which all mankind have inherited from him.

His description of man's evil heart in the seventh chapter of Romans has already been quoted at length (p. 23f.). In that passage, however, he does not suggest the origin of this evil tendency, though he does link it with the notion of death: 'Wretched man that I am! Who will deliver me from this body of death?' (Rom 7.24). Death, therefore, for him, as for the author of Wisdom, stands not only for the separation of body and soul, but also for a state of sinfulness (cf. Rom 7.9-10). The source of this spiritual death is Adam, just as the source of spiritual life is Christ:

As in Adam all die, so also in Christ shall all be made alive (1 Cor 15.22).

Paul enlarges upon this contrast between the work of Adam and Christ in Romans 5.12-21. The thought in this passage is disconnected and hard to follow, but the main point of the argument stands out clearly in the central verses (18-19):

Then as one man's trespass led to condemnation for all men, so one man's act of righteousness leads to acquittal and life for all men. For as by one man's disobedience many are made sinners, so by one man's obedience many will be made righteous.

48

Thus St Paul treats of Adam's disobedience, which made all men sinners, simply in order to show how Christ's obedience made all men righteous. The argument proceeds *a fortiori*: Christ's obedience achieves 'much more' than Adam's sin (5.15, 17).

In an interrupted sentence at the beginning of this section St Paul brings in the notion of death:

As sin came into the world through one man and death through sin, and so death spread to all men because all men sinned... (5.12).

In the light of the passages we have already examined (Rom 7.24; 1 Cor 15.22) it is safe to conclude that here too 'death' denotes spiritual death or sinfulness as well as physical death.

What is not so clear, however, is what St Paul means by saying, 'All men sinned'. The interpretation that prevailed in the West from the late fourth century to long after the Council of Trent was that Adam's sin *ipso facto* made all men sinners. The passage seemed to teach this doctrine of inherited sinfulness with even greater cogency, because the Greek phrase (*eph' hōi*) translated 'because' was mistranslated in Latin *in quo*, and taken to mean 'in Adam'; all men became sinners in Adam, i.e. by virtue of his act, not their own.

The correct translation of the phrase is usually taken to be 'because', though 'so that' is a plausible alternative. The first supposition does not demand any particular interpretation of the words 'All men sinned'. The meaning could be that Adam's sin introduced spiritual death (the evil heart?) into the world, but death was able to spread only because the rest of the human race also chose to sin; this would be a doctrine of imitation of Adam's example. But the passage could mean that this death was able to spread to all men because they were tainted with Adam's guilt – a doctrine of inherited original sin.

If, on the other hand, *eph' hōi* means 'so that', the

49

thought of the passage progresses as follows: Adam's sin introduces death (sinfulness) into the world, which spreads to all men so that they all in their turn, like Adam, choose to sin. In this case St Paul is teaching a doctrine of an inherited tendency to sin (evil heart).

There are, therefore, three possible interpretations of the passage:

(1) Adam was the first to sin, and we sin by our own choice, like him (inherited example);

(2) Adam's sin makes us sinners, whether we choose to sin personally or not (inherited guilt);

(3) Adam's sin bequeaths us a legacy of 'death', the 'evil heart', which leads us to sin personally too (inherited tendency to sin).

What we have seen of the background of Jewish thought might lead us to expect that (1) or (3) is most likely to be correct. The logic of the whole section, however, favours (2). St Paul is not saying that Jesus' obedience empowers us to make similar acts of obedience and so gain life and righteousness; the life and the righteousness are free gifts, undeserved.

While we were enemies we were reconciled to God by the death of his Son (Rom 5.10).

Consequently if the comparison is accurate it ought to mean that it is Adam's disobedience, not our choice, that makes us sinners. Our sinfulness and our righteousness both derive from another.

This doctrine of inherited guilt seems severe. To get it in proportion we must remember that Paul teaches it simply in order to explain Christ's munificence in redeeming us. We did not deserve to receive grace; we were not even blank canvasses, ready for God to paint. Christ died for us 'while we were yet helpless... ungodly' (5.6); 'while we were yet sinners' (5.8); 'while we were enemies' (5.10). When children are baptized and receive grace long before they are capable of personal sin, if

50

grace is always reconciliation, as St Paul implies, it must be reconciliation after inherited sin. But even if St Paul knew nothing of infant baptism, it still makes sense for him to say: grace comes always in the form of forgiveness and new life for sinners, not only because we all choose to sin, but because we are all tainted with Adam's sin. 'God has consigned all men to disobedience *that he may have mercy on all*' (Rom 11.32). 'The scripture consigned all things to sin, *that what was promised to faith in Jesus Christ might be given to those who believe*' (Gal 3.22). 'Where sin increased, *grace abounded all the more*' (Rom 5.20).

To sum up the whole of this chapter, in both the Old and the New Testament it seems to be taught that subsequent generations inherit the effect of an ancestor's sins. At first the effect is thought to be mainly material; hardship and physical death. But before the end of the pre-Christian era the spiritual meaning comes to the fore: the 'evil imagination' is sometimes considered to be an inherited weakness, at other times emphasis is rather on the freedom with which men choose to sin. It is probable, however, that St Paul went further and held that we inherit from Adam not only a tendency to sin but a state of guilt.

CHAPTER III

TRADITION

(1) *The age of the Fathers*
It is at first sight surprising that the early Fathers of the Church, up to about the middle of the second centu-

ry, while presenting a rudimentary doctrine of original sin do not link it with the first man. Clement of Rome, for example, speaks about man's 'evil heart' (or envy) and alludes to the passage in Wisdom describing the entry of death (Wis 2.24). Referring to the disordered Corinthian church, he writes:

> Righteousness and peace are banished: everyone abandons the fear of God and his faith is dimmed... Each walks according to the desires of his 'evil heart' and assumes an unjust and godless envy, through which 'death entered into the world' (1 Clement, 3.4).

This passage is typical of the thinking of all the Apostolic Fathers: Adam is allotted no part in the origin of the evil heart and the entry of death. This inclination to evil is part of man's inevitable condition; death, both physical and spiritual, is brought on by each man's sin. It is true that Clement is thinking of an historical first entry of death; but when he comes to explain what he has in mind in the following chapter he does not go back any earlier than the sin of Cain.

Three of the writings of this period explain man's evil tendency by a theory which has affinities with the explanation of the *Community Rule,* and perhaps even derives from it (see p. 46). This is the theory of the 'Two Spirits' which prompt man to good and evil respectively. The *Shepherd* of Hermas, an allegorical work which was probably written in Rome in the first half of the second century, speaks not only of two spirits, but also of two 'angels', two 'powers and energies', two 'ways' and two 'desires' (*Mand.* 5.1; 6.1,2; 12.1). The *Didachē,* a composite second-century practical manual, and the *Epistle* of Pseudo-Barnabas, which is of similar date, adopt the terminology of the two 'ways'. For the *Didachē* they are the ways of Life and Death (1.1); Barnabas, on the other hand, calls them the way of Light and the way of

52

Darkness or the way of the Black One (18; 20). But in none of these three sources is there any link with Adam.

On reflection this omission need cause no surprise. In the last chapter we saw the Wisdom books, the Jewish Apocrypha and the Dead Sea Scrolls make much of the 'evil heart' and the spread of death, but do not think it necessary to make Adam the cause of man's sad condition; at most he is the first of a series of sinners. St Paul makes Adam responsible at least for the spread of spiritual death, but it took some time for this idea to permeate Christian thinking. For naturally his epistles were not immediately thought of as Scripture. They achieved this status by the end of the second century, and had begun to be collected even in the first century, but evidently some aspects of his teaching, such as Adam's role in the Fall, took time to be assimilated.

When we come to the Greek Apologists, however, in the second half of the second century, we can see that St Paul's ideas have had time to penetrate. The sin of Adam and Eve is a necessary stage in the spread of evil through the world, but at the same time the responsibility for sin rests with each individual. St Justin, for example, who was martyred about 165, combines these two explanations:

> We know that [Jesus] did not come to the river [Jordan] because he needed to be baptized, or needed the Spirit to descend on him in the form of a dove. Nor did he undergo his birth and his crucifixion for his own needs, but for the sake of the human race, which from the time of Adam succumbed to death and the serpent's trickery, while each member of it indulges in evil *through his own fault* (*Dialog.* 88; PG 6.685).

Justin is the first to elaborate the resemblance between Eve and Mary: the virgin Eve conceived the serpent's word and gave birth to disobedience and death; the virgin Mary obeys the word of the angel and gives birth to the one who brought release from death (*ibid.* 100; PG 6.712). But even in this passage it is clear that Justin is not maintaining that Eve's sin is imputed to her posterity; the sinners of subsequent generations are rather those who imitate the serpent. He puts the same point in another way, when he speaks of

> men who were born like God free from suffering and death on condition that they kept God's commandments...; *in imitation of Adam and Eve they bring death on themselves* (*ibid.* 124, PG 6.765).

When Justin, therefore, thinks of the responsibility of Adam and Eve for our sin, he means simply that subsequent generations re-enact the sinful choice of their first parents; he even appears to maintain that pain and physical death are the consequence of each individual's sin.

To correct the perspective, however, it must be added that Justin seems to introduce Adam and Eve as an explanation of the existence of sin simply as an *argumentum ad hominem* in his *Dialogue with Trypho,* who was a Jew; in his two *Apologies,* which were written to convince a pagan audience, he explains sin almost without reference to the Fall story of Genesis 3.

This insistence on the power of each individual either to make himself a partner in Adam's sin or to reject it and so escape the spiritual consequences is typical of the Greek Apologists. It reappears, for example, in Theophilus of Antioch, who died some twenty years after Justin:

> Just as man through his disobedience brought death on his own head, so it is in the power of anyone who wishes to obey God's will and so gain for himself eternal life (*Ad Autolycum,* II 27; PG 6.1096).

Theophilus, however, makes an original contribution to the interpretation of the Fall: Adam was not a superman, richly endowed with spiritual as well as material favours, but an 'infant'. He should have grown slowly to maturity, remaining like a child submissive to God's commands; but he refused to remain as a child and rebelled against God's prohibition of the fruit of knowledge. It was this disobedience that brought him suffering and death (*ibid.* 25; PG 6.1092).

Several modern writers have noted the emphasis the Greek Fathers place on the freedom each generation has to subscribe to Adam's sin or repudiate it. They contrast it favourably with the Latin teaching which culminated in the severe doctrine of St Augustine and passed into the official thinking of the Western Church. In fact the 'traditional Catholic expression' which has been expounded in Chapter One is to a large extent that saint's thought.

At first Augustine took a much gentler view of original sin. In his polemical writing against the dualistic determinism of the Manichees, who held that the evils of human existence were attributable to an Evil Principle, just as the good in life is due to a Good Principle, St Augustine stressed the power of man's free will to overcome the effects of Adam's sin (*de libero arbitrio*, 3.55; PL 32.1297); babies, having no free will, cannot sin (*ibid.* 3.68; PL 32.1304). In this he was not far removed from the ideas of the Greek Apologists. But reflection on his long drawn-out conversion convinced him that what was all-important was not man's efforts but grace. Now the greater the depths into which man is sunk by sin, the more generous and the more powerful God's grace is shown to be. It is, therefore, with serene faith and love that the saint could write these sombre words as early as 396:

> From the time when our nature sinned in paradise,... we have all become one lump of clay, a lump of sin (*massa peccati*). Since, then, by sinning we have forfeited our merit and God's mercy is

withdrawn from us so that we sinners are owed nothing but eternal damnation, it is pointless for a man from this lump to reply to God and say: 'Why did you make me like this?' (*de div. quaest. LXXXIII*, 68.3; PL 40.71).

Every member of the human race becomes sinful because he possesses a tainted nature, just as every pot made from a lump of poor quality clay will be defective.

This very insistence on the sovereignty of grace stimulated a reaction. Pelagius, the moral reformer from Britain, as all moral preachers must, used to remind his congregations that they could put their lives right if only they chose to do so. St Augustine's insistence on the need for grace seemed to Pelagius likely to weaken people's efforts to reform their lives; Pelagius' insistence on man's power to achieve self-perfection seemed to Augustine a denial of the need of grace. The last thirteen years of the saint's life were spent in controversy with Pelagius and his disciples. To safeguard the all-importance of grace, he was paradoxically forced into a more and more sombre view of the fallen state of man. His developed teaching can be summarized as follows:

Every human being that comes into this world, before he sins of his own free will, possesses the 'defect of his origin, which makes him guilty'; he has within him the 'law of sin', which involves true guilt and is not just a tendency to sin or a punishment for someone else's sin. All men sinned 'in' Adam; all are indentified with him; all are therefore born for damnation. This can be explained in two ways.

(1) Human nature is a unity, a single lump which is condemned *en masse* so as to become a *massa perditionis* through the sin of the head of the race. This truth can be expressed by other metaphors: each human being is saddled with the debt incurred by Adam; the whole race is an organism which is

infected by the corruption which attacked its root. (2) Because of the wound Adam inflicted on human nature, conception cannot take place without passion. This passion is so closely associated with sin that every child conceived in it is under the devil's power. Jesus was free from original sin precisely because he was not conceived by sexual intercourse.

Whatever the explanation of the source of this hereditary taint, St Augustine was clear about the consequences. Our Lord said, 'He who is not with me is against me' (Mt 12.30). Therefore before baptism even a baby is liable to damnation; this is why infant baptism is so important, and is accompanied by various rites of exorcism. 'If a child is not rescued from the power of darkness but remains there, why should you be surprised that he will be with the devil in eternal fire?' (*Op. imperf. contr. Jul.* III. 199; PL 45.1333). Exclusion from the kingdom of God is a severe penalty, but not so severe as to make our Lord's words apply to unbaptized babies: 'It would have been better for that man if he had not been born' (Mt 26.24). Such babies are genuinely punished, but with 'the lightest condemnation of all' (*Contr. Jul. Pelag.,* V xi.44; PL 44.809; cf. III iii.9 and V. i.4; PL 44.706, 784).

Baptism, St Augustine taught, releases us from the guilt (*reatus*) with which we entered the world, but the consequence of this guilt remains. This is the tendency to sin, which the saint calls 'concupiscence', and which is most apparent in the sexual passions; in the baptized, however, it does not of itself involve guilt. There are other aspects of man's depravity which also persist even after baptism: man remains subject to ignorance, pain and death. Adam, on the contrary, had been a superman, with the highest intellectual endowments as well as freedom from bodily afflictions.

The contrast between the views of St Augustine and those which can be found in the writings of the Greek Apologists can be analysed as follows:

(a) Augustine: Adam was a superman who fell. Apologists: Adam was a child who developed on the wrong lines.

(b) Augustine: subsequent generations are implicated in Adam's guilt because they share his nature. Apologists: subsequent generations are free to associate themselves with Adam's guilt or not.

It has become fashionable for writers to generalise this contrast into one between the severe Western view and the optimistic Eastern view of original sin. That St Augustine's theory forms a natural culmination of Latin thought since the time of Tertullian is true; the need to fight Pelagianism only darkened his picture of man, but did not change its essential outlines. But it is much less accurate to regard the Apologists' position as representative of Eastern thought. Since this misconception is not uncommon today, it will be worth devoting some space to showing where it fails to do justice to the facts.

The Apologists' position is restated with greater clarity by St Irenaeus (c. 140-c. 202), and for that reason is sometimes called the 'Irenaean' view. According to him Adam and Eve were like children, with the sexual innocence of the young. They were not naturally immortal; immortality was a gift of God which they could either accept or reject. They were made in God's image, and as they grew in maturity, they were to become more faithful images of him; but, being childlike, they fell an easy prey to the serpent's deceits. Yet Irenaeus believed that, for all his immaturity, Adam was highly gifted in more than one way: above all, he possessed the gift of the Spirit, which he forfeited by his sin not only for himself, but also for his descendants, and which Christ restored.

Irenaeus, like the Apologists, believed that subsequent

generations could recover what Adam had lost. In this life, he thought, they can recover a progressively greater share of the Spirit; but it will not be until the final restoration of creation that they will regain some of the other original gifts, such as mastery over the world. Yet although Irenaeus in this way underlines man's power to use his free will in order to receive the Spirit, his position is quite different from the one which Pelagius later assumed. For Irenaeus believed that the Spirit is entirely God's gift, made possible only by the Incarnation, though man is free to accept or reject it; whereas Pelagius held that man's efforts alone were sufficient to recover what was lost, once Christ had provided an example.

Thus Irenaeus clarified the Apologists' teaching concerning Adam's original immaturity and the power of all men to recover what Adam lost. But in one fundamental point Irenaeus departs from the so-called 'Irenaean' position: he teaches that we all share Adam's sin. Basic to Irenaeus' thought is the belief in the solidarity of the human race; he expresses this in Pauline terms by stating that all men sinned 'in' Adam. However, he retains St Paul's optimism: what we lost in Adam is restored to us in Christ.

When (the Word) became incarnate and was made man, in his own person he recapitulated in summary the whole length of human history and made salvation available to us, so that what we lost in Adam – our existence in the image and likeness of God – we might recover in Jesus Christ (*Adv. Haer.*, iii. 18.1; PG 7.932).

Whether this solidarity with Adam is a share in the guilt of Adam's sin, or only the punishment or effects due to it, Irenaeus does not explain. But what justifies his description as an optimist is his belief in the power of our solidarity with Christ to cancel out, with plenty to spare, the effects that we share with Adam. He does not, however, discuss how and when this salvation is applied to each individual; he leaves, therefore, untouched the question of the state of the unbaptized which so darkened the thinking of St Augustine.

Many of the other Greek Fathers, such as Clement of Alexandria and Gregory of Nyssa, similarly express belief in Adam's 'childishness' and our power to regain what he lost. There will be no need to indicate these ideas in the thinking of each author. What is needed, rather, is the counterbalance of the other, less optimistic, ideas which they adopt; in this way one may hope to show that the contrast between the Western and Eastern positions is less marked than many allege.

That Colossus among the Fathers, Origen of Alexandria (c. 185-c. 254), produced a great range of bold speculation on the subject of original sin. He saw that the account of Adam's fall in Genesis is not simply literal history but is what we have called 'myth': an account in symbols of the human condition. Nevertheless, he did believe in a Fall, though he saw several possible interpretations of the doctrine. In an early work he suggested that each individual soul had fallen in an earlier, disembodied existence, and he seems never to have completely rejected this view. In later writings, however, he gives a theological interpretation of Genesis 3 based on the supposition that the events there recounted are historical. He did not decide between the several ways in which all mankind shares Adam's sin. Is it because Adam contained in his body the seeds of all the future race, just as Levi was contained in Melchizedek's loins, and so can be said to have received tithes from Abraham (Heb 7.9-10)? Or because the human race, which, once redeemed, becomes Christ's Body the Church, before redemption is what St Paul calls a 'body of sin' (Rom 6.6, not RSV), i.e. a society united by its sinfulness? Or because conception made the offspring spiritually unclean, as the OT purifications show? All these suggestions presuppose a sinfulness coming 'from birth' or 'from the seed'; but it also is passed on 'from training', i.e. by environment as well as heredity. We choose to contribute to the race's sin: 'it was not without our co-operation that death established its reign over us' (*Commentary on Romans*, V; PG 14.1024). Yet babies already share in this sinfulness before they can co-operate with it freely; this is why infant baptism is practised.

Origen seeks confirmation for his belief in the spiritual corruption even of babies from such texts as the following:

Behold I was brought forth in iniquity,
   and in sin did my mother conceive me (Ps 51.5).
Let the day perish wherein I was born
   And the night which said,
   'A man-child is conceived' (Job 3.3; cf. Jer 20.14-15).
For who is clean from stain?
   There is no-one (Job 14.4, translated from Septuagint).

He notices the use of the word 'stain' rather than 'sin' in the third of these passages, and seems to take the distinction in the sense in which later theologians distinguished between original and personal sin. Babies carry the stain, not the sin; but even so they need to be baptized 'for the forgiveness of sins' (*Homilies on Luke*, xiv; PG 13.1834-5). Even Jesus carried the stain, because he had a real human body. (Other Fathers after Origen were to infer the existence of original sin from the fact that babies are baptized 'for the remission of sins'.)

Another great Father of Alexandria, Athanasius (295-373), teaches the solidarity of man like his compatriot Origen, though his speculations do not range so widely. As a result of Adam's transgression *we* become

lost, naked, earthy, defective, imperfect, maimed, in
debt. Adam extinguished the life in human flesh, so that
its properties now are corruption and sin. By 'sin'
Athanasius means personal sin; by 'corruption' he seems
to mean moral corruption, though whether this is inherited guilt or inclination towards sin is not clear. The incarnate Word restores man to incorruptibility by water
(baptism) and the Holy Spirit. Like Origen, however,
Athanasius pays little attention to the unbaptized.

Yet another Alexandrian, Didymus the Blind (313-
398), who was inspired by Origen and like his master
was made instructor of the catechumens of that city, expresses with greater clarity the distinction between personal and inherited sin. Commenting on the text: 'If I
am wicked, woe to me! If I am righteous I cannot lift up
my head' (Job 10.15), he writes:

> Perhaps he means something like this: If I sin from
> choice, woe to me! If from Adam's transgression
> and the debt which is handed on to us by succes-
> sion, again I shall not be able to lift up my head as
> one freed from every stain. For some sins owe their
> existence to our own choice, and are followed by
> *punishment;* others to our ancestors and will re-
> quire *purification (Commentary on Job;* PG
> 39.1145).

A new-born baby is only potentially good or evil, and
realises this potentiality only when it is old enough to
know what it is doing. In other words, we inherited a moral
defect which causes shame and needs purification, but
this in itself does not make us evil.

The fourth-century Cappadocian Fathers have their
own way of expressing mankind's share in Adam's sin.
The most common formula is the use of the first person
pronoun in reference to Adam and his descendants:

> *We* were once in glory when *we* lived in Paradise,
> but *we* became inglorious and humble because of

the fall (Basil, *Commentary on Psalms,* 114.5; PG 29.489).

I wholly fell and was condemned because of the disobedience of the first man and the deceit of the adversary (Gregory of Nazianzus, *Oratio* 22, 13; PG 35.1145).

Gregory of Nazianzus faces the problem of little children who die without baptism. They are not punished, because they are not wicked; they have suffered harm, not done it. But they will not share eternal glory: 'for it does not follow that anyone who does not deserve punishment deserves reward' (*Or.* 40, *On Baptism,* 23; PG 36.389). All the same, the saint believes it is better not to baptize a baby at once, but to wait till the child is about three, when it will have some little understanding of the sacrament (*ibid.* 28; cf. 17).

Many of the Greek Fathers speak of the inclination to evil that results from the Fall. Another Cappadocian, Gregory of Nyssa, speaks of it as a sympathy (or instinct, *sumphuia*) for evil in the soul which corresponds to the body's mortality. Gregory seems to connect it with the passions; he does not wish to confine his thought to sexual passion, though he believes that all the passions are rooted in the sexuality with which God equipped man even before the Fall, but in anticipation of it.

The great Father of Antioch, John Chrysostom (c. 354-407), similarly believed that man began to experience the passions because of the Fall; he indeed goes further, and says that before the Fall there were none. Originally man experienced an urge upwards towards God, but Adam's sin forfeited this for the whole race. Chrysostom is the first of the Fathers to attempt to think out an answer to the question: 'How can Adam's sin make his descendants sinners?' To be a sinner, he answers, in this context means to be punished, not to be guilty; and

63

if it seems unjust to be punished for another's guilt, one can reply:

We are so far from taking any harm from this death and condemnation, if we are sensible, that in fact we have gained by becoming mortal: first because we do not sin in an immortal body [note the implication that the body is more responsible for sin than the soul]; secondly, because we are afforded much matter for philosophical reflection *(Commentary on Romans, x; PG 60.478)*.

As an additional reason the saint adds the possibility of a meritorious death like that of a martyr. But his solution in fact does not answer the question he set himself: to say that death is beneficial does not explain how it is a just *punishment*.

Many of the Greek Fathers, beginning with the Apologist Theophilus of Antioch (died c. 185), in order to illustrate how death is beneficial in healing man's hereditary defect, compare the human condition with a flawed vase. In Theophilus' version of the parable, the vase which has to be broken up and remoulded illustrates man's defective state, which can be put right only when he is dissolved at death and rises again immaculate. In the third century Methodius of Olympus gave a new twist to the illustration by applying it, not simply to man, but to the body in particular. It is in the body that sin is implanted; the body must therefore be broken up and reconstituted.

Another attempt to clarify the question was made by a contemporary of St Augustine's, Mark the Hermit. What we have inherited from Adam, he maintains, is not his sin, because in that case we should all be born sinners, which is not true. What we inherit is his death, which consists in separation from God.

This survey should have made it clear that the commonly alleged contrast between the 'Augustinian' and the Eastern views is a distortion of the truth. Both traditions, in fact, show a considerable measure of agreement over the following basic points:

1) Adam's sin involved his descendants in physical effects like liability to death.

2) It involved them in an inclination of the will and the feelings away from the good.

3) Man's freedom, co-operating with grace, is able to overcome this evil tendency.

4) Besides this tendency to sin, man is born with the heritage of something akin to guilt, which is not the same as personal guilt. This formulation occurs in several Eastern as well as Western Fathers, though some prefer to speak of something like absence of the Spirit rather than guilt.

5) Christ has redeemed us from this inherited deficiency.

6) Representatives of both traditions agree that for the unbaptized this deficiency is not supplied.

Two other conclusions seem justified. The first is that the optimism of the Greek Apologists undergoes considerable modification in the later Greek Fathers. The second is that the difference between the Greek and Latin Fathers seems to be one of emphasis and emotion rather than belief. At the risk of oversimplification it might be said that the typical Latin attitude is: 'Alas for the evils into which we are born'; while the Greek reaction is rather: 'Thank God for the privileged state to which Christ has restored us.'

(2) *The Council of Trent.*

A book of this size must inevitably settle for omissions if at least the salient points are to be adequately treated. For this reason it is necessary to skim rapidly over some 1100 years and pick up the threads again at the Council of Trent.

In 418 the Council of Carthage enacted several canons to rebut the Pelagian errors. In connection with original sin, the canons condemned the following beliefs:

1. That Adam would have died whether he sinned or not;

2. That babies are not baptized for the remission of sins, and do not contract original sin from Adam.

3. That there is an intermediate state for unbaptized babies between hell and heaven (Dz 222-4).

The condemnation of these propositions follows the mind of St Augustine. This explains the condemnation of the third proposition, for, according to his thinking, there is no state of purely natural sinlessness: one is either saved by God's grace or a sinner without God's grace. Unbaptized babies, therefore, must be in hell. (Paradoxically, many modern theologians argue from the same premiss to the opposite conclusion that unbaptized babies must go to heaven.)

The second Council of Orange (A.D. 529) carried the definitions of Carthage a stage further. As a result of Adam's sin his descendants suffer death and sin (death of the soul). In addition their free will is weakened (Dz 371-2, 378).

These two councils were regional, not general, but their decrees were confirmed by popes and became generally accepted in the Western Church. As Western thought continued to clarify, a distinction was made between the two main spiritual effects of Adam's sin: first, the loss of original justice; secondly, concupiscence or the weakening of the will. The first of these effects entailed what could be described as a state of sin or guilt, and the absence of sanctifying grace; it was put right by baptism.

The great scholastic doctors differed in the emphasis they placed on these two effects. St Anselm of Canterbury (d. 1109) took the essential element to be the state of nakedness without due justice, which is brought about by Adam's disobedience and turns everyone into 'children of wrath' (*De conc. virg.*, 27; PL 158.461, quoting Eph 2.3).

In other words the lack of grace is not merely the absence of a possible perfection, but the deprivation of something which ought to be present. By this loss we are separated from God. This state can be called a sin, but differs both from personal sin and Adam's sin: Adam's sin arose from his own choice, the inherited sin arises from 'natural necessity' (*ibid.* 22-3). The tendency to sin is a consequence of the Fall, but is sinful not of itself, but only as long as it is accompanied by the absence of grace (just as the same remark is either an insult or a mark of friendship according to the speaker's disposition). St Thomas Aquinas stated a similar theory when he said that the principal or formal element of original sin is the absence of the state of justice in which man was originally created, so that the will is turned away from God; the consequential or material element is the disorder of the faculties which tend away from the good (*Summa,* la 2ae, q. 82, art. 3). Henry of Ghent (d. 1293), however, following an exaggerated Augustinian tradition, taught that original sin consisted essentially in the inclination to sin which arose from the union of the soul with an infected body. William of Ockham (d. 1349), on the other hand, reacted in the other direction and eliminated concupiscence from his definition of original sin altogether, making it consist solely in the lack of original justice.

The fullest official definition of the doctrine is contained in the decree on original sin passed in the fifth session of the Council of Trent (1546) (Dz 1511-16). Its six canons can be summarized as follows:

1. Adam by his sin lost 'sanctity and justice', incurred God's anger, became subject to death and

the devil's captive. He was thus affected in both body and soul.

2. These consequences affected also his descendants: i.e. the loss of sanctity and justice, the physical effects like death, and 'sin, which is the death of the soul'. Rom 5.12 is quoted in support of this view.

3. Adam's one sin is communicated to his descendants 'by propagation not imitation', so that it belongs to each individual. It cannot be removed by human effort but only by the redemption won by Christ. This restoration is applied by baptism to both adults and babies.

4. The baptism of babies, even those of Christian parents, is a legitimate and necessary practice, and remits sin in them, namely the original sin they contract from Adam.

5. Through the grace of Christ conferred at baptism 'the *guilt* of original sin', which has the 'true and authentic nature of sin', is removed. It is not that this guilt simply ceases to be 'imputed'; there remains in the baptized 'no condemnation' (cf. Rom 8.1) to keep them from heaven; they become renewed and innocent. Concupiscence, however, remains in the baptized. It is a challenge rather than a source of harm, and in the baptized is called 'sin' not literally but because 'it comes from sin and inclines to sin'.

6. The above is said without prejudice to belief in the Immaculate Conception.

Although the Fathers at Trent thought fit to reaffirm the teaching of Carthage and Orange against the Pelagians and semi-Pelagians (see p. 66), their intention was not to provide a complete statement of Catholic teaching, but to expound this teaching on points which the Reformers had questioned; five of these six canons, in fact, take the form of condemnations of heretical propositions, sometimes with reasons added. In order to understand the mind of the Council it is necessary to know something of the heresies that were being denied. We are fortunate, therefore, in possessing a list of these heresies that was compiled at the Council; the following is a summary of this list, with an indication of the canons in which each heresy is condemned. The attribution of the heresies to their alleged proponents is not always just; but, *for the understanding of the mind of the Council,* what matters is what the heretics *were thought* to hold.

1. Pelagius: We were not born sinners; we contract no stain from generation. Condemned in canon 3.

2. Manichees, etc: Those born in Christian marriage do not contract original sin. Condemned in canon 4.

3. Pelagians and Erasmus: Romans 5 does not teach original sin. Condemned in canon 2.

4. Pighius (a contemporary Dutch Catholic theologian): Original sin does not belong to each individual, but God imputes it to each (i.e. by a legal fiction the sin is 'deemed' or 'counts as' ours). Condemned in canon 3: 'it belongs to each individual (*unicuique proprium*)'

5, 6. Luther: The concupiscence which remains after baptism is all that is meant by original sin, and is identical with sexual concupiscence. Condemned in canon 5.

7. Pelagius: Original sin is the bad example of Adam's sin, which we imitate [just as he held that Christ redeemed us solely by his teaching and good example, not by communication of grace]. Condemned in canon 3.

8. Pelagius, Luther: The baptism of babies is not necessary as a means of expiating original sin. Condemned in canon 4.

9. Pelagius, Luther: Unbaptized babies are neither damned nor belong to the Kingdom of Christ; but they are saved and possess eternal life (cf p. 66).

10, 11. Anabaptists: Infant baptism is invalid. Condemned in canon 4.

12. (No attribution): All the acts of an unbaptized child are sins. It was apparently not considered necessary to condemn this heresy explicitly.

13. (No attribution): There is not one original sin. (Presumably a Pelagian theory, implying that each has only his own personal sins). Condemned in canon 3.

It is surprising that such a small proportion of the canons is intended as a rebuttal of Martin Luther's position. The first four are all largely anti-Pelagian; it is not until the fifth that the thought reaches anywhere near the heart of Lutheranism. It will be well, therefore, to devote a little space to a slightly fuller exposition of his views.

As he had developed his theological thought within the order of the Augustinian Friars, it is no surprise that he claimed to derive many of his leading ideas from his patron. Like Augustine he painted a dark picture of the effect of original sin on the race only to offset it with a serene belief in the resources of God's mercy and the redemptive work of Christ. Each member of the race, because of Adam's sin, possesses a 'corruption of nature...' the secret, root-sin... which bears the fruit of evil works and words' (Weimar ed., 8. 104-5). This secret sin is a state of sinfulness, rather than an act, and reveals itself in a lack of faith and in concupiscence or radical selfishness. Our individual sinful actions are simply practical realisations of this basic state.

Original sin, then, Luther taught, is a genuine corruption, which persists even after the sin is remitted. Justification (the forgiveness of sin) follows faith; that is to say, when sinful man trusts in the mercy of God, God does not heal the corruption of sin, but, by a sort of legal sentence, no longer imputes it to the sinner, and instead imputes to him the righteousness of Christ.

> God does not consider a man to be just because he *is* just; a man is just *because* God considers him just... Is he therefore perfectly just? No, he is at the same time a sinner and just (*simul peccator et iustus*); a real sinner, but just by the imputation and certain promise of God *(Commentary on Romans,* Weimar ed., 56.22,272).

Therefore good works do not save a man; nothing can avail to save him except faith.

Against Luther's teaching, the Council of Trent declared that at baptism man ceases to be a sinner and becomes righteous in fact and not simply by imputation, for the concupiscence that remains after baptism is not itself sinful. In the following session the point was developed in the decree on justification:

> By the merit of the most holy passion through the Holy Spirit the love of God is poured out in the hearts of the justified and *inheres in them* (Dz 1530).

In its deliberations on original sin the Council took no cognizance of the teaching of Calvin, perhaps because there were so few French bishops present. Calvin, like Jansenius in the following century, placed the essence of original sin in concupiscence, which persisted after baptism as a corrupting force. In this the Reformers, and even more, Jansenius, claimed to be following the teaching of St Augustine: but this interpretation gives an incomplete account of the saint's thought.

The decree of the Council of Trent became normative to Catholic thinking; the condemnation of the positions of Baius and the Jansenists in the sixteenth to eighteenth centuries simply reinforced the Tridentine doctrine. Pius

V, for example, in 1567 condemned the following propositions of Baius:

The integrity [i.e. freedom from concupiscence] of the first creation was not a gratuitous elevation of human nature, but its natural condition. The immortality of the first man was not the free gift of grace but his natural condition (Dz 1926, 1978).

In 1794 Pius VI condemned a more comprehensive decree to the same effect that had been passed by the Jansenistic Synod of Pistoia (Dz 2616). Baius and the Jansenists considered the present human condition so corrupt that it was sub-human; by his nature, they taught, man is immortal and free from concupiscence. The Church's teaching, however, was that man's original immortality and integrity were free gifts of God which man has forfeited, thus reverting to his natural concupiscence and mortality.

There remains space for only the briefest glance at subsequent developments. In 1854 Pius IX defined the doctrine of the Immaculate Conception:

The most Blessed Virgin Mary in the first instant of her conception was preserved immune from all stain of original sin by a unique grace and privilege from almighty God, in consideration of the merits of Jesus Christ, the Saviour of the human race (Dz 2803).

In 1950 Pius XII, in the encyclical *Humani Generis* attacked polygenism (cf. p. 30):

The faithful cannot accept this theory... since it is by no means clear how such an opinion can be reconciled with the teaching of the sources of revealed truth and the decrees of the Church's magisterium on original sin, which proceeds from a sin truly committed by one man Adam, is spread to all by generation, and is in each individual as something personal (Dz 3897).

72

The condemnation, it will be noted, is qualified; the pope does not say polygenism is false, but that there does not appear to be any way of reconciling it with the doctrine of original sin. More recent papal statements similarly decline to advance beyond the Tridentine definitions.

In this chapter we have recorded and sometimes discussed various moments in the development of the Church's doctrine of original sin. In our choice, we have selected, not only the key-documents, like the decree of Trent, but the theories of the Fathers which help to illustrate the course of the development or to correct misconceptions. This has been necessary in order to correct the common misrepresentation of tradition and to provide a means of assessing more recent theories. But in so far as it is legitimate to speak of the overall pattern, the doctrine emerges in a form which hardly goes any of the way towards meeting the four types of objection discussed in Chapter 1. We must now turn therefore to modern attempts to re-interpret the doctrine in a more acceptable form.

CHAPTER IV

THE MEANING OF THE DOCTRINE

(1) *The 'sin of the world'*

The traditional interpretation of the doctrine of the Fall and original sin is open to many objections, some of which we have discussed in Chapter 1. To the modern mind perhaps the most damning objection is simply that the doctrine is irrelevant: I just can't believe, people feel, that what Adam did can make any difference to my life.

The first step towards the rehabilitation of the doctrine is the realization that the account of the Fall in the third chapter of Genesis is not literally accurate as history or science. It is a theological account, in the form of a 'myth', of the way in which the sin and evil in the world has come into being, not from God, but as a result of man's free decision and the decision of his ancestors (see p. 38). St Paul, in his turn, uses the same myth to illustrate the truth that all salvation comes from the one Man, Christ (see p. 49).

St Paul's use of the myth does not guarantee its literal truth. It used to be put forward as an exegetical principle that, although one was not justified in insisting in a thoroughly fundamentalistic way on the *literal* truth of every passage in scripture, *the sense intended by the author* was always guaranteed from error. On this principle it would follow that the interpretation of the Genesis account which St Paul accepted is true. It might be that he quoted it as a useful illustration, while recognizing that it was not historical. Or it might be that he used it as an illustration without deciding in his own mind whether it was literally true or not. In either case the literal truth of the story of Adam's fall would not follow. But if St Paul himself believed it to be literally true, then it must be so.

But this method of exegesis is too narrow. It is possible that a biblical author, who uses an Old Testament story as an illustration of the gospel message he wishes to convey, accepts this story uncritically as the literal truth when in fact it is myth. One can perhaps see a similar situation in Our Lord's use of the story of Jonah:

As Jonah was three days and three nights in the belly of the whale, so will the Son of Man be three days and three nights in the heart of the earth (Mt 12.40).

It may be that Jesus is using the story of Jonah as an illustration though he knows it is not literally true. It is

74

possible that he uses it in this way without considering whether it is literally true or not. But one should not exclude a third alternative: that, although he mistakenly believed it to be the literal truth, his primary concern was not with the Jonah story but with his own resurrection which he was using the myth to illustrate. Whichever of these three possibilities is true, we are not justified in appealing to the inerrancy of scripture as evidence for the literal truth of the story.

So too, even if St Paul believed that the story of the Fall in Genesis was a piece of literal history, it would not follow that he was right in this belief; for the gospel-truth that he is teaching here is the universality of the salvation won by the work of the one Man Christ. The inerrancy of the Bible means that the gospel message a passage proclaims is true; but it does not imply that the terms in which this message is couched are the only terms possible, or that they have a validity in their own right. Revealed doctrine can develop; that is to say, the presuppositions and concepts according to which a doctrine is formulated can be discarded and the doctrine reformulated in other terms. It is possible that a biblical author may not distinguish in his own mind between message and presuppositions. But the presupposition is *not* the message. Accordingly we need not scruple about counting ourselves wiser than St Paul in this respect; whatever he may have thought about the Genesis Fall-story, respect for the Bible does not compel us to believe in its literal truth.

Many Catholic theologians in the last few years have consequently felt free to construct a bold reinterpretation of the doctrine. Among them are A. Hulsbosch, P. Schoonenberg, A. Dubarle, P. de Rosa and the authors of the 'Dutch Catechism'. Naturally each writes with his individual nuances, but it is possible to state a common position without doing an injustice to any one of them.

Such Protestant theologians as C. H. Dodd speak in similar terms.

The doctrine of the Fall, they would agree, is not about man's origins but about his present condition and his future. Man is unperfected: he is capable of evolving to a more advanced state, which includes a development in his social responsibilities. He is also imperfect: collectively and individually he has not reached the stage of evolution which it was in his power to reach; in other words, man has sinned. Man's progress is free; but the very gift of freedom makes sin a possibility and therefore, statistically, inevitable. Sooner or later someone would sin, and initiate a false path of evolution. The Yahwist had not learned to think of the world in evolutionary terms. Therefore the only way in which he could conceive of this incompleteness and deficiency in man was to say that man's present state is below the state in which God created him rather than the state to which God destined him to evolve. Paradise represents man's potentiality, not his past.

Each individual sins personally, and so fails to fulfil his moral potentialities, and to that extent checks and deflects the process of evolution. But we are not simply individuals. Our progress is conditioned by the choices of others. From the very beginnings of our consciousness we are under pressure from society to sin, and all too soon we yield to this pressure and contribute to the undoing of others. Sin grows like a snowball.

Moreover, no man is an island. We are not individuals who happen to have relations with others; our relations with others constitute what we are. We find ourselves in a selfish, divided society, and inevitably ourselves become selfish and out of harmony with our fellows.

Our membership of this sick race is not something that seems to us morally indifferent. It is a source of shame to us, just as we would feel ashamed if a member of our family had been justly disgraced. This feeling sometimes takes the form: 'There but for the grace of God go I'; we recognize in ourselves the urge which could lead us to commit the sin we can see in others. At other times we feel responsibility for the injustice of society; that some men are born doomed to poverty because of their class or their country; that a man can be hated and oppressed because of his race; that Christians cannot unite. Our society is to blame for these injustices, and therefore we feel a share in the guilt.

This sense of social guilt and this downward drag of society on the individual, of course, affect his relationship with God. The second great commandment, to love our neighbour, is inseparable from the first. In so far as we are at odds with society, we are impeded from loving God. If we are dragged down by society to selfishness and injustice, we are dragged away from God. Original sin, therefore, is our membership of a society which prevents us from loving God and our neighbour as we ought. But however divided we may be from our society by our selfishness, we are united with it in this: we freely yield to society's pressure and contribute to it ourselves. 'Each of us is an Adam for himself' (see p. 47).

When St John the Baptist pointed out Jesus, he said: 'Behold, the Lamb of God, who takes away the sin of the world' (Jn 1.29). The word 'sin' is singular, although the Roman liturgy uses the plural (*qui tollit peccata mundi*). The implication is that the world's sinfulness is more than the sum of each individual's personal sins; it is a gigantic group-factor, like the emotion of a mob which is something more than the sum of the reactions of each individual. The sin of the world is a collective will in which I am a partner, a pressure by the group on the individual which I share and to which I contribute. The sin of the world is original sin.

If this interpretation is adopted, there is, of course, no

need to defend monogenism with all its difficulties. Just as the Fall is a myth, so descent from Adam is a myth. One need not even argue that monogenism is false: it is simply irrelevant. We are all members of the same guilty race whether we have all descended from a single ancestor or not.

(2) *Separation from God*

The explanation that has been expounded in the first section of this chapter has much to commend it. It is supported by one interpretation of the scriptural texts; it sounds reasonable, and finds an echo in human experience. But there is one more test which it does not pass so well: does it do justice to tradition?

There are, in fact, three ways in which the Church's teaching seems to indicate that this account of original sin is incomplete:

(a) The Council of Trent distinguished between two elements in original sin: the guilt, which is sin properly so called, and is remitted at baptism; and concupiscence, which remains after baptism. But the 'sin of the world', as it was expounded above, remains in the baptized, for they are still subject to the influence of sinful society. What then is the 'sin' which is forgiven through baptism?

(b) The definition of the dogma of the Immaculate Conception stated that our Lady was by virtue of a singular privilege immune from original sin from the first moment of her conception (see p. 72). If original sin is the pressure of society on the individual, it is hard to see how she could have been immune. Even if she was brought up by saintly parents, and so did not suffer from her contact with them, how was she cocooned from pressures outside the family? And if such insulation is possible, why does it not happen more often? Why should the children of saints not be similarly free from original sin?

(c) Trent asserted against the Pelagians that original

sin is transmitted 'by propagation, not by imitation' (see p. 68). Pelagius had held that Adam's influence on his posterity was psychological; his choice influences our choices. Trent, on the contrary, taught that original sin is more fundamental, something earlier and deeper than the psychological influences that play on me from my earliest childhood. It is with me 'from propagation'. Although many of the bishops at Trent exaggerated the function of the body as the medium by which original sin is inherited, this last phrase should not be taken as the canonization of the patristic theory that the physical process of conception or the passions attendant upon it cause original sin. It had been rejected by St Thomas (*Summa,* 1a 2ae, q. 81, art. 1), and the Council was most careful to avoid condemning orthodox Catholic teaching, like that of Aquinas. 'From propagation' must mean 'from the beginning of my human existence, by the very fact that I am human, even before any psychological influences have come to bear on me'.

These three difficulties are all solved if we add depth to the definition of original sin. It is not only my entry into membership of a sinful society; it is my entry *without grace.* This absence of grace is a fact from the first moment of my existence even before the evil influences of my fellow-men can corrupt me; it is therefore due to propagation, not imitation (objection c). Our Lady, on the other hand, was full of grace from the beginning, but this privilege had nothing to do with insulation from human influences (objection b). This lack of grace is supplied by baptism, though concupiscence remains (objection a).

One should not, of course, think of grace as a *thing,* a possession, which is absent from every human being until he is baptized. Grace is God's gift of himself to the person (uncreated grace), and the enhancement (created grace) of the person's own powers to know and love

79

God, so that he shares in the divine nature, and God's gift becomes part of him ('inheres': see p. 71). When grace is explained in these terms, a question at once arises: How could a newly-conceived human being possess grace? How can the absence of this grace constitute a genuine lack in the embryonic human being? What could be the meaning of created grace in a baby who is totally incapable of knowing and loving anybody? What could be the meaning of uncreated grace in a baby who is totally incapable of forming a personal relationship with anybody, let alone God?

The answer must be that, though grace is manifested on the psychological level, it cannot be reduced to a mere psychological capacity. However unformed his mind, the baptized baby is included within the Covenant, is taken into a relationship of love with God, in a way which is not true of the unbaptized. This relationship implies more than external membership of the Church. It entails God's self-gift, i.e. uncreated grace. As the child develops it will receive that degree of created grace of which it is capable. This presence of grace will eventually be manifested as faith, hope and charity in the conscious life of the growing person; but the reality of grace is there in the baptized even before it can emerge into consciousness. (Of course, the unbaptized can come to love the God he does not consciously acknowledge, and so, by 'baptism of desire', be filled with grace as an 'anonymous Christian').

The absence of grace in each new human being is not our punishment for the sins of our ancestors; such punishment, it was argued in Chapter 1, would be unjust. Nor is it the result of an arbitrary decision on God's part: 'I will endow them with grace on condition that no one sins'. God has, of course, the *right* to make such a contract, but the all-good and all-wise God cannot act by whim. If he did grant the human race grace under such a condition, it must be because the condition is reasonable.

That it is reasonable follows from man's social nature and from his ability and duty to co-operate with divine providence. (1) Man's need for society is not verified only at the microcosmic level of the family, the group of friends or the team collaborating to achieve a common good. Unless we suppose God to be without reason in his arrangements, the Mystical Body of Christ, the Communion of Saints, must correspond to the social needs of man's nature. For some purposes the whole of the human race is a single society; the biblical doctrine of corporate personality cannot be totally demythologized. It is only because of this solidarity of mankind that the saving work of Christ redeems the whole race. Here again it seems unworthy of God to act in an arbitrary manner: it seems more reasonable to regard the redemption not simply as the Father's forgiveness of the human race because he is won over by the loving obedience of his Son, but rather as a process of reconciliation and restoration which takes place in the one person of Jesus and which therefore reconciles and restores the whole race *because of the solidarity of the race*. Jesus is the representative man: in St Irenaeus' phrase, he 'sums up' in his own person all human history.

St Paul regards Jesus as the second, not the first representative man. The first was Adam: Jesus is 'the last Adam' (1 Cor 15.45); later writers have preferred to call him 'the second Adam'. St Paul argues from the then accepted fact that all died in the first Adam to the conclusion that all are made alive in the second Adam (1 Cor 15.22). In the twentieth century we perhaps need to reverse the logic; the fact that all were made alive in Christ shows that it is reasonable to maintain that all 'died' (i.e. were born without grace) in Adam – provided we understand 'Adam' not necessarily as a single historic individual but a symbolic figure standing for the whole race.

It perhaps helps to illustrate the point if we compare this solidarity of the race in original sin with our share in the responsibility for other situations which we did not create. I did not cause the divisions in the Church: I did not distribute the world's wealth unfairly. But I share the guilt for the sinful situation. I can free myself from the guilt only by trying to correct the abuse; if I do nothing I am adding my signature to the injustice, and therefore become doubly guilty.

(2) Moreover, God requires us to co-operate with him. The Incarnation required May's *'fiat'*; biblical inspiration requires the author to use the ordinary human means of literary composition; God uses human beings as instruments to bring others to believe in him. Karl Rahner suggests that this last point applies to God's gift of grace to each new human being. This can only happen with human co-operation: 'only a *whole* sinless original group can transmit grace to its descendants' (*Concilium,* vol. vi, June 1967, p. 34). Rahner here speaks only of an *original* sinless group, but the same point would apply to any group: only the sinless group (or family?) can produce children endowed with grace.

It still remains to be shown how this absence of grace can be accurately described as sin, as Trent maintained. The Council distinguished between the 'guilt' of original sin, which is sin properly so called, and concupiscence, which is not (Dz 1515). Evidently the Fathers at Trent believed that both of these categories of 'sin' were distinct from personal (actual) sin, at least in so far as the voluntary element is concerned. St Anselm had said that Adam 'sinned of his own will', his descendants contract original sin 'by natural necessity' (*De Conc. Virg.* 23). St Thomas similarly calls original sin 'a sin of nature' (*Summa,* la 2ae, q. 81, art. 1).

There are two reasons why this lack of grace can properly be called sin. The first is the solidarity of the race that has just been discussed: we share in the guilt of the race, just as we share in the redemption of the race. The second reason is that the effect is the same as the effect of sin: alienation from God. This was one of St Augustine's most valuable insights: there is no middle state between friendship with God (i.e. grace) and separation from him; 'He who is not with me is against me'. There is no merely natural moral perfection. In other words, absence of grace is not the absence of an optional adornment, it is the frustration of the capacity of our natures to share the divine life. (This point will be discussed at greater length in *The Theology of Grace* in this series.) We are like engines overheating because the gears are not engaged. We came into this world, then, as members of a sinful race, equipped for union with God but separated from him.

Grace first comes to us, then, as the reconciliation of a sinner, not a free gift to a deserving recipient.

> One will hardly die for a righteous man – though
> perhaps for a good man one will dare even to die.
> But God shows his love for us that while we were
> yet sinners Christ died for us (Rom 5. 7-8).

Even before I have made any choice of my own, I need to be redeemed. Consequently, our Lady's preservation from original sin was an act of *redemption;* she was redeemed from the sin of the race from the very first moment she belonged to it.

(3) *Concupiscence, death and suffering*

This explanation of original sin given so far has not yet accounted for the origin of the psychological and physical elements or original sin, namely concupiscence, death and suffering. We must consider them now.

So far we have not given any precise definition of

concupiscence. The reader will probably have noticed that in fact the word has been used in more senses than one. It can mean:

a) The sexual instinct, with or without the accompanying passions.

b) The passions in general. (Is this what St Paul meant by 'the law of sin which dwells in my members': Rom 7.23?)

c) Our basic selfishness. This does not consist exclusively or even predominantly in our sensitive appetites or emotions. It is much deeper, an inclination of the will. Our wills are divided between selfishness and love.

d) The innate tendency in man towards what he sees to be desirable. This tendency operates on the level of the will as well as of the sensitive appetite, and is logically necessary for any human choice. It is not, therefore, something evil, and is in no sense the result of the Fall. This basic neutral appetite corresponds closely with the basic human drives in some modern psychological theories: the *id* (Freud), the aggressive instinct, the group mind.

e) (K. Rahner's definition) A resistance in ourselves to our own decisions, which prevents us from ever throwing in the full weight of our will behind them. We can only make the most trivial decisions without any holding back. It is, therefore, an inability to be wholly absorbed in the good, but it also operates for the good, preventing us from giving ourselves wholly to what is evil, as when we blush to tell a lie. This is the weakness of will that St Paul complains of: 'I can will what is right, but I cannot do it' Rom 7.18). It was in these terms that the Decree on Justification of Trent spoke of concupiscence. 'Free will was certainly not extinguished in them, though it was weakened and biassed' (Dz 1521).

All but the third of these experiences seem to be part of man's natural make-up. Not only is it impossible for us to imagine human existence without them; this alone would not prove that man could not be without them. But there is no need to imagine man without them, as they are not evil. There is nothing wrong about the sexual and other passions, and man's basic drive towards the good; they are good in themselves. Even what we have called weakness of the will is not in itself evil; for it is hard to see what moral growth or development in character would be possible if the will were completely integrated. It is only in heaven or hell when all growth is completed that the will is focussed wholly on a single object. Moreover, the 'physical' and 'moral' objections of Chapter 1 are relevant again: if man were originally without concupiscence, how could the sin of Adam upset this psychological balance in his descendants; and if God himself disturbed this balance, how could this be just? The third type of concupiscence, on the other hand, is something which seems to come from personal choice rather than heredity. I am born with concupiscence in sense d), but this is morally neutral, proper and inevitable self-regard rather than selfishness. But I make myself into someone who is concupiscent in sense c), i.e. genuinely selfish.

If this is so, it seems that in none of these senses is concupiscence the inherited result of a Fall. Nevertheless Trent says it is accurately described as 'sin', though not in the literal sense, because 'it comes from sin [Adam's, presumably] and inclines to sin' (see p. 68). It is easy to see how concupiscence in senses d) and e) inclines us to sin, for without it we would not be able to sin at all. Besides, my experience of concupiscence is inextricably mixed up with my consciousness of sin, so that I reasonably project the notion of sin on to concupiscence itself, and exclaim with St Paul, 'Wretched man that I am!

85

Who will deliver me?' (Rom 7.24). In other words, the fact that concupiscence bewilders me and inclines me to sin comes itself from sin, my own sin; and as concupiscence makes me vulnerable to the downward pressure of society, its power derives from the sin of the world. I can never love as much as I would like to love, and this fact makes me feel guilty. I am right to feel guilty about this disability because I know only too well that it leads me to sin and makes me vulnerable to the sinful society I live in so that I become fully one with this society. And all of this is true although concupiscence in itself is necessary and morally neutral. But we have still to account for the Church's teaching that Adam before the Fall enjoyed integrity, not as a natural property but as a privilege. Perhaps the doctrine can be best interpreted in this way: Before sin entered the world, man was in a state of grace. As a consequence of this union with God, concupiscence did not appear as a consequence or a cause of sin, for there was no sin in man's experience. It was simply part of man's make-up, which man turned to good. It was because of the privileged possession of sanctifying grace that man did not know concupiscence as an evil.

Physical death, too, it seems, is a necessary stage in human existence; partly because the body must wear out some time, and partly because it is only by death that we can pass from what has traditionally been called the wayfarer's or pilgrim's state in this life, when we are able to grow morally by our choices under grace, to the state of permanence in heaven or hell, when we can no longer grow by making new decisions which involve the love or the rejection of God. In what sense, then, can it be said that it was man's sin that made him mortal?

The solution that we have just suggested for the problem of concupiscence seems to apply again here. Man always was, and necessarily is, mortal. But in our sinful society we do not regard death as the end of a pilgrimage to be welcomed with serenity, or as the achievement of the last stage in our moral growth. Rather, death frightens; or death is an escape; or death is a fate to be accepted stoically. The humanist who advocates euthanasia perhaps imagines himself walking with dignity off the stage of life into the void of non-existence. But the instinct of self-preservation is so strong that, when it comes to it, few die so ideally. It is hard to regard death as anything but an evil, or at best an escape, particularly if one does not believe in a resurrection after it.

It is sin which makes death, like concupiscence, seem something evil. Our personal sin and the sin of our society poison our relationship with God. We cling to the values of life and it causes us pain to relax our grip. We are not in a fit state to face the justice of God, and we do not trust him enough to rely on his mercy. 'The fascination of wickedness obscures what is good, and roving desire perverts the innocent mind' (Wis 4.12). Man has always died, but it is sin that makes death seem an evil. Only the saint can regain the attitude of innocence to death, like St Paul, who declared: 'My desire is to depart and be with Christ' (Phil 1.23).

The same can be said about pain. Sin did not change man's physical structure so as to make him sensitive to pain. Man was always liable to it, but it is not in itself an evil. Pain is morally neutral; it can be a challenge, and we can grow in courage, generosity and sympathy by meeting it. 'Everything works for good with those who love God' (Rom 8.28). It is sin that turns pain into an object of fear, an obstacle to love, a trial to faith.

(4) *One Adam*

There is one element in the decrees of Trent which it may be felt has received cavalier treatment here: this is the apparent insistence on the historic reality of the 'first

87

man Adam'. The reader may indeed suspect that I have been using Trent to suit my own preconceptions, insisting on those parts of the decrees which confirm my argument, ignoring those other parts which contradict it. It will be well, therefore, to make a few remarks about the use the Catholic theologian ought to make of the documents of the magisterium. The presupposition that has been accepted in this chapter is that dogmas develop: they need to be re-thought and reformulated in contemporary terms. What part do the Church's definitions play in this process of rethinking?

One can err by neglect or by over-reliance. The first error is the more popular one today. Sometimes it appears that the reason for it is simply a contempt of history, but a theological justification might be given. As doctrines develop, the teachings of the magisterium constitute the Holy Spirit's guidance for the Church *at that time;* these definitions of doctrine help the Church's thought to grow in the right direction, but then become irrelevant. The Church has to be guided by scripture and the Holy Spirit as he speaks in the Church *today.* Such a justification of the neglect of earlier teachings of the magisterium cannot, however, be accepted by a Catholic, as it amounts to a denial of the doctrine of Tradition.

The contrary error is that of over-reliance, the uncritical acceptance of the literal meaning of each part of a dogmatic definition as a truth of faith. It has rightly been pointed out that it is inconsistent to reject fundamentalism in the exegesis of the Bible while insisting on a fundamentalist interpretation of the Church's definitions of dogma. The same interpretative techniques apply in both areas. In particular, the remarks that were made earlier in this chapter about the need to distinguish between the essential saving message and the author's presuppositions and illustrations apply to the utterances of the magisterium as well as to the Bible. The form in which definitions are framed often makes this distinction hard to draw: for example, when a heretical proposition is condemned, does it follow that the contradictory proposition is declared to be an article of faith? Or is the heresy not the content of the proposition but the heretic's denial of the Church's right to legislate in the matter? For example, in Trent's condemnation of an heretical view of marriage, such as:

If any one says that matrimonial cases do not concern ecclesiastical judges, let him be anathema (Dz 1812),

the subject-matter, the competence of ecclesiastical courts, concerns discipline not revelation; the question of heresy comes in only because the Church's authority is denied.

In interpreting the Tridentine decrees on original sin, we are fortunate in possessing a means of avoiding the fundamentalist mistake. The Council Fathers did not intend to give a complete exposition of the doctrine. We should not look to them for guaranteed answers to questions which had not been asked in their time. Their aim was to show where Catholic teaching differed from that of heretics. Therefore the list of heresies on original sin which they drew up (see p. 69f.) shows us what they regarded as the essential elements in their own teaching. Chief among these heresies were those of the Pelagians and the Reformers. Neither of these parties had called in question the historicity of an individual Adam. The Council Fathers, therefore, did not consider discussing the point; they simply took it for granted and uncritically accepted the biblical myth as historic fact. So although, if asked, each of them would have said that he took belief in an historic Adam to be an article of faith, this does not constitute part of the essential teaching of the Council. The decrees of Trent do not rule out the belief that 'Adam' is a myth symbolizing the human race, any more than St Paul's apparent literal acceptance of the myth in Romans 5 compels us to follow him.

Neither faith nor reason, then, compels us to believe that all men are descended from the one original sinner. It is not certain, however, what is required in order that all should share in the social guilt of the race. Some would say it is necessary that all should be descended from an original sinful group. But it seems more likely that biological descent is not the source of human solidarity, and that there is no need to postulate an original representative group in whose sin we all share; the fact that the human race has become a race of personal sinners is enough to explain why every member of it is born alienated from God.

(5) *Summing-up*

Every human being is a member of a race of sinners. When he comes into this world he is already estranged from God, and immediately becomes subject to influences which urge him still further away from God. He becomes aware of the weakness of his will and the strength of his passions, which again lead him to sin. He faces the prospect of death, which he sees as the loss of all the worldly values he has come to cherish. All of which is simply to say that he shares in original sin.

Christianity is a religion of redemption. I constantly need to be redeemed from my personal sins. I needed to be redeemed from my estrangement from God with which I entered the world. But original and personal sin are each a *felix culpa*. Sin puts us in a new relationship with God. Our love of him gains a new dimension. Instead of self-approval, we have to rely on his loving forgiveness.

Where sin increased, grace abounded all the more, so that, as sin reigned in death, grace also might reign through righteousness to eternal life through Jesus Christ our Lord (Rom 5. 20-21).

A man who had enjoyed many years of married life once said: 'When a man first falls in love with his wife, everything is marvellous. But it is only when they have learnt to forgive each other and ask for forgiveness that they really learn what love is.'

ON BOOKS AND SOURCES

General

P. Schoonenberg: *Man and Sin* (London, Sheed and Ward, 1965, p.b.)

Part I

L. Monden: *Sin, Liberty and Law* (London, G. Chapman, 1966)

Part II: Chapter 2

A. Dubarle: *The Biblical Doctrine of Original Sin* (London, G. Chapman, 1964)

J. de Fraine: *Adam and the Family of Man* (New York, Alba House, 1965)

Chapter 3

A. Gaudel: 'Péché Originel' in *Dictionnaire de Théologie Catholique,* vol. xii

N. P. Williams: *The Ideas of the Fall and of Original Sin* (London, 1927)

Chapter 4

K. Rahner: 'Original Sin' in *Sacramentum Mundi,* vol. iv

K. Rahner: *On the Theology of Death (Quaestiones Disputatae,* Herder-Nelson, 1961)

K. Rahner: 'The Theological Concept of Concupiscentia' in *Theological Investigations,* vol 1 (London, Darton Longman and Todd, and Baltimore, Helicon, 1961)

K. Rahner: 'Evolution and Original Sin' in *Concilium,* vol. 6, no. 3, June 1967

A New Catechism (The Dutch Catechism) (Burns Oates – Herder, 1967), pp. 259–70

M. Hurley: 'The Problem of Original Sin' in *Clergy Review,* October 1967, pp. 770–786

A. Hulsbosch: *God's Creation* (London & New York, Sheed & Ward, 1965)

In the account of the teaching of the Fathers in *Chapter 3* and elsewhere few references were given. Some readers may be grateful if the most important passages are listed here; for convenience I have generally referred to the Migne editions even where better editions exist.

Justin: *Apology*, I. 10, 28, 61 (PG 6. 340f., 372, 420f.); II. 5 (PG 6.452)

Augustine: *De Peccato Originali*, xxxi.36, xxxix.44f. (PL 44.403,407f.)

    De Nuptiis et Concupiscentia, I.xxiii.25f., xxxii.37; II.v.15, xxxiv.57 (PL 44.428f., 434, 444f., 471)

    De Peccatorum Meritis et Remissione, I.xxviii.55 (PL 44.140f.)

    Enchiridion, 26 (PL 40.245)

    De Civitate Dei, xiv.26 (PL 41.434f.)

Irenaeus: *Adversus Haereses*, III.xx.1, xxii.4; IV.xxxviii; V.vi.1, viii, xii.1, xvi.3 (PG 7.942,959, 1105-9, 1137, 1141-3, 1151, 1168)

    Demonstratio, 12, 37

Origen: *De Principiis*, I.viii.1; IV.iii.1 (Koetschau, pp. 94ff., 323ff.)

    Commentary on Romans, III.3; V (PG 14.933, 1003-56)

    Homilies on Leviticus, VIII.3 (PG 12.496)

    Contra Celsum, I.32; IV.40 (PG 11.721-4, 1093-6)

Athanasius: *Oratio adversus Arianos*, II.61, 65; III 33f. (PG 26.277, 285, 393-7)

Didymus: *Commentary on 1 John* (PG 39.1792)

Gregory of Nyssa: *Oratio Catechetica*, 8 (PG 45.33-7)

    De Hominis Opificio, 17f. (PG 44.188-96)

Chrysostom: *Homilies on Genesis*, II.xv.4, xvi.5 (PG 53.123, 131)

Theophilus: *Ad Autolycum*, II.24-27 (PG 6. 1089-96)

Methodius: *On the Resurrection*, i.41-3 (Bonwetsch, pp. 285-91)

Mark the Hermit: *De Baptismo*, PG 65.1017

gnosticism 9
grace 17-21, 24-5, 50-1, 55-6, 65-7, 72, 79-83, 86, 90-1
  inherent 71, 80
Gregory of Nazianzus, St 63
Gregory of Nyssa, St 60, 63, 94

Henry of Ghent 67
Hermas 52
Hilary, St 28
Holy Spirit 58-9, 62, 65, 71, 88
Hulsbosch, A. 75

image of God 58-9
imitation *see* exemplar
immortality 29, 34, 39, 43-6, 58, 64, 72
integrity 25, 34, 72, 86
Irenaeus, St 58-60, 81, 94

Jansenius 71-2
Justin, St 53-4, 94

Koestler, A. 10
Leeming, B. 26-7
limbo 26-7, 66
Luther, M. 69-71

Manichees 9, 55, 69
Manual of Discipline see *Community Rule*
Mark the Hermit 64, 94
Mary and Eve 53-4
  Immaculate Conception 68, 72, 78-9, 83
Methodius of Olympus 64, 94
monogenism 30, 78
myth 34-5, 60, 74, 78, 89-90

natural law 16
Newman, J. H. 9

Ockham, W. of 67

Orange, Council of 66, 68
Origen 28, 60-2, 94
pain 24-5, 28-9, 35, 38, 44, **54**, 57, 87
passions 63, 84-5, 90
Paul St 46-51, 74-5, 81, 87
  Romans 23-4, **47-51**, 68-9, 83-6, 90-1
Pelagianism 28, 56, 58-9, **66**, 68-70, 78-9, 89
Pighius 69
Pistoia, Synod of 72
Pius V 71-2
Pius VI 72
Pius IX 72
Pius XII 72
polygenism 30, 72-3

Rahner, K. 82, 84
Robinson, H. Wheeler 36

Schoonenberg, P. 75
serpent 35, 53-4
sex 34-5, 57-8, 63, 69, 84-5
sin, act/state 19-20
  personal 9-11, 13-21, 82, 87, 90
  mortal/venial 17-20
  objective/subjective 16, 18-20
  unforgivable 17-18
  original *passim*
  how propagated 27-8, 57, 79; *see* conception
solidarity 15, 23, 35-6, 38, 56, 59, 61-2, 76-9, 81-3, 86, 90

Tertullian 58
Theophilus 54-5, 64, 94
Thomas Aquinas, St 67, 79, 82
toil 24-5, 34-5
Trent, Council of 19, 49, 65-73, 78-9, 84-5, 87-9
Two Ways or Spirits 46-7, 52

First published in the Netherlands
Made and Printed by Van Boekhoven-Bosch N.V. - Utrecht